GET IT

GET IT

FIVE STEPS TO THE SEX, SALARY AND SUCCESS YOU WANT

AMYK HUTCHENS

This publication is designed to provide helpful information in regard to the subject matter covered, but it is not a replacement for professional resources. It is sold with the understanding that neither the publisher nor the author are engaged in rendering legal, accounting, or psychiatric counseling services. If legal advice or other professional assistance is required, the services of a competent professional person should be sought. As with any self-development type resource, your results may vary. Your results will be based on a wide spectrum of variables, including, but not limited to: your level of effort, emotional intelligence skills, communication skills, and a myriad of other factors. Since these factors differ for each individual, we cannot guarantee your success, results, or profitability; nor are we responsible for your success or failure in getting what you want. The author simply and sincerely hopes that you do get your wants for making the world a better place for all, including you. In order to maintain the anonymity of the characters in these stories, the names of individuals have been changed as well as some identifying characteristics and details such as physical properties, occupations, and geographical locations.

GET IT

Five Steps to the Sex, Salary and Success You Want

ISBN   978-1-5445-0693-7 *Hardcover*
       978-1-5445-0691-3 *Paperback*
       978-1-5445-0692-0 *Ebook*

FOR WANTERS EVERYWHERE

CONTENTS

INTRODUCTION

"It was either you or Sal," said the voice on the other end of the phone.

"Who's Sal?" I asked.

"The divorce attorney."

* * *

People do not call me when their lives are hunky-dory. They call me when they are at their wits' end and not even remotely close to getting what they want.

"My spouse wants to go on vacation—without me. I want this relationship to work. I really do. And I want more sex."

"My kids are selfish and self-absorbed and only call me when they need a ride, money, or both. I want my kids to be more polite. I want to be appreciated."

"My business partner is planning a surprise coup—and surprise, I know about it. I just want peace. And a new partner."

"My brother's a narcissist—and, not so ironically, he wants our mom's antique mirrors. By the way, she's not even dead yet. I want him to be respectful. And to get facial warts. Big ones."

"My boss is insane. He doesn't care that he calls me at three a.m. with questions that can wait until eight. I want to be successful, but this is nuts. I want to make a ton of money without enduring this bullshit."

"My team is inept. My overhead is killing me. I want to quit and do something more enjoyable. Seriously, I want to walk out tomorrow and never look back. "

"My husband's ex-wife is unhinged. She plays psych games, talks to me like I'm an idiot, and pits the children against us. I want her to stop treating us like we're the enemy. I want to stop giving in to her bad behavior."

"I swear, if I see one more get-rich-quick idiot reach ten

thousand followers before I do, I will scream. Out loud. I want a better brand presence. And I want people to stop telling me to work smarter, not harder. It doesn't work. Working smarter is not working. Nothing is working! How the bleep do I get what I want?"

If you're wondering if you can really get what you want, there's good news. You can. And it's easier than you might think, and, bonus, not illegal. But it is a skosh radical and uncomfortable. And it works. It really works.

After twenty-eight years as a teacher, trainer, business consultant, coach, and award-winning international speaker, I have repeatedly proven in my own life and the lives of my clients that there are four core tenets about what it really takes to get what you want. Once you take on these four game-changing truths as your own, you will begin to get exactly what you long for, and it will feel downright magical. It will be as if someone gave you a powerful wand and taught you how to cast some phenomenal spells.

THE FOUR TENETS OF GETTING WHAT YOU WANT

1. Life happens one conversation at a time.
2. The quality of your life is a direct reflection of the quality of your conversations.
3. The life you desire is on the other side of a tough conversation.

4. Tough conversations, navigated successfully, get you what you want and create the profitable life you desire.

Booyah! You get what you want one profitable conversation at a time. Once you "get" that your life is happening one conversation at a time, with yourself and with others, then you can actually get "it"—the life you desire. Knowing these Four Tenets and applying the forthcoming Five Steps are life changers.

As you will see, your toughest conversations will almost magically become far less daunting and far more lucrative. The proven steps I'm sharing work. Full stop. Thousands of individuals and teams I've worked with throughout my career have turned their toughest conversations into their most profitable ones. You will too. That's why I'm super excited that you've got your hands on this book. These charmed steps will have you confidently and competently navigating your way through your most critical conversations so you can create the life you desire and get more of what you want, starting today.

IMAGINE

Suppose in this crazy, complex world you could start every day with a confident smile...knowing every tough conversation at work and at home would ignite an "aha" moment and get you the results you desire? Guess what:

you can. And all it requires is one significant adjustment to *how* you play this game called life.

Begin by picturing your typical frustrating conversations at work. You know, all those tension-laden talks about shrinking sales, zero accountability, mediocre marketing campaigns, salary freezes, operational inefficiencies, lackluster team members, dwindling cashflow, and disgruntled clients. Too often in these conversations you get swept up in the energy of others whose sole goal is to vent, whine, blame, and rehash. In order to stay sane and keep your left eye from involuntarily twitching midmeeting, you mentally check out. While people are complaining, your mind wanders to inane yet safe subjects, such as how the word *stressed* spells *desserts* backwards. You're thinking, *Wow! How did I not notice that before now? It can't be a coincidence.* Your craving for cake instantly increases as a colleague delves into yet another increasingly less tasty morsel of dissatisfying discussion.

Next, recall your challenging conversations at home. From missed curfews, trespassed boundaries, overflowing trash bins, and sex (or the lack thereof), to loading the dishwasher improperly and cray-cray family members. These touchy topics, along with many others, create so much tension in you that even a full-size foam roller, a bottle of wine, and a handful of muscle relaxants would have a hard time loosening the knots in your neck.

These wearisome conversations are often so stressful or downright painful that, instead of preparing for them, you find it best to try and avoid them at all costs. Which, unfortunately, means you're still not getting what you want. But you *are* getting fed up with life and a tad resentful of all the energy sucks.

ABRACADABRA

Now, imagine that you suddenly possess a realistic yet magical wand that fully comprehends the Four Tenets and knows how to apply the Five Steps for getting what you want. This wand is so brilliantly powerful it's capable of completely turning all of your tough conversations into highly profitable ones, both at home and at work. From passive-aggressive neighbors to manipulative teens and everyone in between, this wand starts delivering the precise results you desire every time you wave it. People start treating you respectfully. Money starts to flow in and stay longer. Meetings are suddenly productive problem-solving sessions, and that putz in procurement actually helps you close the deal. Wait, what? Could it be true? Oh yes. This wand inherently knows exactly how long you've not gotten what you want and the cost of not getting it. Even better, this wand understands exactly what it would mean to you to get what you desire. It also understands the impact it would have on your life when you finally get what you want. Could such a magic wand really exist?

Indeed, it does exist, and it won't be just a hypothetical illusion for much longer. It's about to be your new reality. Your prized possession. You will own this realistic magic wand and wield it well.

If you've been looking for a fresh, straightforward, brilliant way to better navigate the critical conversations in your life without saying something you'll regret, giving your power away, or damaging your relationships along the way, you've finally found it!

The steps, insights, and magical phrases shared inside this book will show you exactly how you can get your heart's desires and change your life forever. All of the tough conversations mentioned above are from real-life clients who simply didn't possess the benefit of savvy communication skills. The wand you're about to possess is spectacularly magical when you know exactly *how* to use it.

The five-step approach laid out for you in this book will make you instantly smarter about how you problem-solve and interact and engage with others, and it will make you far more masterful and compassionate about how you talk to yourself. In other words, it's as close as you'll get to casting spells of enchantment in the real world.

But first, if you're wondering whether you really need this wand and its five-step magic, here's a question for you.

If, starting today, you were a better problem-solver, a better decision-maker, a more thoughtful communicator and collaborator, and a more confident, high-performing action-taker, what results would you see six months down the road?

Yes, exactly!

That's the power of profitable communication skills and knowing exactly *how* to get what you want. That's the power of the wand. And if you thought you could get what you want without it, think again.

As a matter of fact, think about this:

> Tough conversations are attempted and avoided every single day, and yet, the life you desire is on the *other* side of these tough conversations. Which means, the longer you put off learning exactly how to successfully conduct tough conversations, the longer you put off living your best life at home and at work. Simply put, the longer you live not knowing how to communicate your needs and ask for what you want, the longer you put off getting what it is you truly want.

On average, each day you engage in six to nine significantly meaningful conversations that will influence your future. Relationships with colleagues, family members, neighbors, your partner, and even yourself are filled with tough conversations. When these tough conversations are navigated successfully, they become highly profitable conversations and yield the results you desire.

Every raise, promotion, relationship, friendship, deal won, or course corrected—that is, every milestone EVER accomplished—happened one conversation at a time. Your very existence started with a conversation: "Hi." (And maybe a good cologne.)

Your voice, your brand, your business, your family, your legacy is built one profitable conversation at a time. Hear me now: *the life you desire* is created one conversation at a time. Imagine all the profitable outcomes you can potentially produce when you lead brilliant, kick-ass conversations. Yep, that's what I'm talking about. You're about to strike conversational gold.

Waiting until the "timing is right" to ask for what you want means the timing is wrong. Using your voice to course correct yourself or someone else before a series of transgressions occurs can prevent a whole lot of pain from unfolding in your life. Your mantra for dealing with what you *don't* want in your life is now *the sooner the better.*

Tough conversations will occur in your life with many different people at many different times, and some of the toughest conversations will be the ones you have with yourself. This manuscript is the ultimate self-help book because it contains the exact techniques I used to help both myself and my clients. They say that necessity is the mother of invention, and there was a painful time in my life when I desperately needed what I invented in these Five Steps.

Years ago, I found myself lying on the floor, tears silently streaming down my cheeks, my body pulsing from real, vibrant, clean pain when I started asking, *How did I get here? Where did this series of events begin?* Maybe it was my inner knowing who answered with *When you compromised here; when you caved a little there; when you settled for this, that, and him; when you people-pleased last Monday and were too bitchy last Friday; when you drew a boundary, but in the wrong place at the wrong time; when you let yourself be a doormat at the wrong entry; when you said no instead of yes or maybe when you meant hell no while simultaneously smiling and nodding...or maybe it was fifteen years ago when you simply didn't know better.*

But what if that voice was just my inner critic? The fault-finding voice that experiences fear and lack of self-confidence and often requests unattainable perfectionism? What if the very first thing I needed to do was change my internal dialogue? What if I needed to hush my inner critic and bolster up my inner champion?

It was on that day, in that moment, that I realized if I was going to be where I longed to be, where I'd envisioned I'd be—and yet oh-so-far from it in reality—then a whole new series of events needed to begin. I needed to rethink, reevaluate, and reset just about...well, everything.

The life I had built, the decisions I had made, were crumbling to the ground, and my identity was erased in a single solitary request from a man I'd been with for twelve years. Four words tilted my axis: "I want a divorce." Fourteen weeks later my husband, our two dogs, our home, our shared possessions, our co-owned business, and our intertwined lives were history. I was living in a new home, sans man and dogs, sans furniture and cars, sans habits and routines, sans titles and roles, sans security, but with a whole lotta pain and debt.

Typically, when we experience a darker period in our lives, irrespective of each individual's details, we will experience Kübler-Ross's famous stages: denial, anger, bargaining, depression, and acceptance. In one of the darkest periods of my life, I leaned into each of these phases instead of resisting them. I spent an extraordinary amount of time journaling and processing my thoughts and feelings. Through each phase I looked at myself

in the mirror, raw and naked, and asked, *Who are you…
really? Who might you be…really? What might you still do…
really?* I didn't rush nor apologize for the phase I was in
on any given day. I didn't force answers when none were
forthcoming. I cried when I wanted to cry, stayed up late
eating chocolate when I wanted to self-soothe. I shut out
the world when it seemed best to not take my wrath out
on innocent others.

And then one day I stopped asking, *What might you still
achieve?* and started asking, *What do I want? What do I
really, deeply, truly want, and how the bleep do I get it?*

I wanted to feel radiant and generous and financially
grounded. I wanted to feel creative and cherished and
significantly meaningful. I wanted inner and outer peace
in my life. I wanted to be surrounded by people I loved
and who loved me back.

This clarity rebuilt me. It was perhaps the most major
reset of my life—philosophically, emotionally, spiritu-
ally, and physically. Leaning into the answers to these
questions—*What do I want? What do I really, deeply, truly
want, and how the bleep do I get it?*—I rebranded my company and my style. I wrote an Amazon best-selling book. I
got involved with nonprofits and formed stronger friend-
ships than I ever had before. I paid off all prior-life debt
and got financially grounded. I discovered my true self

and some pretty cute shoes along the way. Why? Because in order to get what I wanted, I needed to become the person who could feel radiant, generous, grounded, creative, cherished, and significant. I needed to become the person who could create inner and outer peace in my life. I needed to become the person who knew how to be surrounded by people I loved and who loved me back. I wanted to have a bigger, more positive impact in my own life and the lives of others, and the only person who could ultimately give me exactly what I wanted was me. I now, finally and fully, understood that the new me could only emerge when I started engaging in tough conversations instead of shying away from them.

In an extraordinarily painful way (as many of the best lessons in life are served up), I learned that even though these tough conversations can be nerve-racking, the real gain you seek is waiting for you on the other side of the tough conversation. I also learned that I cannot want something for someone else more than they want it for themselves. We must choose for ourselves what we want and support others in their creation of what they want. Figuring out what you want and using your five-step wand is entirely up to you. Creating the life you want will happen one conversation at a time, most especially when the conversation is with yourself. You are the only person who can lead these life-creating conversations.

POWER AND PROFITABILITY DEFINED

Many people crave power and money or profit. Before we go any further, let's define *power* and *profitable* in the context of communication skills and getting what you want. When I use the word *power* (aka the power of using your own voice), it is not about dominion over others. *Power* is about standing up for yourself, honoring your beliefs, declaring your worth, and making your way in this world so you can SHINE YOUR LIGHT and get what you want and need to fuel your light. Damn skippy!

You own and use your *power* both internally and externally. Your internal *power* is about selecting what you believe and perceive, crafting the narrative of the stories you tell yourself and choosing how you talk to yourself. Your internal *power* determines your sense of self-worth, your mental attitude about yourself, and the worthiness of your own voice. Your internal *power* frames how you respond to external conversations. Your internal *power* also gives you bright, crystal-clear clarity on what it is you truly want.

Your external *power* is about consciously choosing your words and your responses so you can better create the life you desire. You can steer conversations toward the profitable outcomes you seek, including, but not limited to, healthier, happier relationships, goals exceeded, deals closed, ideas innovated upon, and your best life lived.

When I use the word *profitable*, it's not just about money. Oh sure, money is one component, but *profitability* can just as easily be measured by your time used wisely, processes streamlined to be more efficient, your energy increased, fewer mistakes made, boundaries established, or even barriers broken down. *Profitability* can ultimately be defined in a myriad of ways once you know how to have the right conversation at the right time in the right way to get what it is you truly want.

Profitability can also be measured by your increased confidence levels. When you master powerful conversation skills, you're less frustrated and more articulate, succinct, strategic, thoughtful, and yes, more sure of yourself. Booyah!

Profitability is also about the dividends you'll yield when you start to feel less intimidated and experience less frustration because your communication skills are KICK-ass. All of which makes your voice stronger.

When you start experiencing the power of *owning your own voice*, you'll more effectively articulate what you want and need, and get what you want and need. Hence, you'll be more influential. When you actively listen, you can respond thoughtfully and wisely and do a much better job of managing yourself and your relationships with others. You'll be more competent, content, and connected. And that's an awesome way to experience *profitability*.

In other words, when you master the answer to *How do I get what I want?* you'll be the very best version of you. You'll be your best self with yourself and with others, and you'll be living the very best version of your life thus far. A bold statement with bold results thousands of people have already achieved from using these tools. Get ready to be your own HERO. Cape not included but encouraged. Or just wear your favorite pair of badass underwear, or just be you, now armed with this astonishingly miraculous wand.

On the occasion when you don't get exactly what you immediately want (like figuring out how to give your obnoxious sibling facial warts), then these five essential steps will challenge you to better understand your underlying needs and find alternative ways to satisfy your deepest longings. With each of the steps, I've included a magical phrase or two. They're designed to be your enchanting responses when you need to handle the tough, awkward, or most important conversations in your life. Let's get started. It's time to get you what you want.

THE FIVE ESSENTIAL STEPS FOR GETTING WHAT YOU WANT

You don't get what you want just because you want it. Wait! Stop! WHAT?! Yep, you heard me. You don't get your way simply because you want it or you know how to throw a really impressive temper tantrum. First, in order to get what you want, you have to effectively learn how to ask for what it is you really want. Second, you are far more likely to get what you want when you understand that behind every surface want, there's an underlying need with a more intense longing to be fulfilled. Third, you cannot wing it when it comes to your wanting, which means you need to prepare and practice using the Five Steps.

It can be a huge struggle to figure out exactly what to do and say to get a critical conversation to go smoothly and ensure you get what you want. Communication is hard. Trust me—I know. I hear your frustrations. I see your anguished eye rolls and feel your clenched jaws. Coworkers, bosses, siblings, friends, kids, spouses, parents, and neighbors all invite you to engage. Some even demand it. And then they challenge you—daily—to respond maturely, wisely, empathically, and resiliently. Many people you meet in your daily life have axes to grind or wounds to heal. They don't want to let you off the hook until they've reeled you in. They are a challenge but not an insurmountable one when you implement the Five Steps for engaging with them.

Getting what you want will require you to up your communication game, but sometimes knowing exactly what to say, when to say it, how to say it, how to keep the conversation on track, heck, how to even get it started, is downright difficult. Knowing how to confidently hold your own so you can create a profitable outcome can be anxiety-inducing, time-consuming, frustrating, paralyzing, and a total soul-suck.

In the end, disastrous conversations can cause you to surrender, fly into a fitful rage, stomp away, sound off, not get the outcome you want, or perhaps just avoid these conversations and this person or people altogether. While these outcomes are far from magical, I get it. Which is why I've taught thousands of people how to overcome their fears and experience the power of using their own voice to get exactly what they desire. When you know how to skillfully lead and steer the toughest conversations in your life, you can:

- Tackle your most challenging problems
- Meet and exceed your goals
- Sell any product, service, or idea
- Connect with anyone

...all while being your best self!

It's a game-changing superpower...that, unfortunately, most people never use. Most people do not get what they want. Most people avoid or poorly attempt tough conversations every single day of their lives. They miss out on fun-loving relationships and greater sex lives, promotions and making more money, pursuing more satisfying and rewarding careers, living an energetic and healthy life, or ever getting to realize their full potential and impact.

You being at your best changes your world. This is why it's so important to know the steps and use your wand to start casting some seriously kick-ass conversation spells. The Five Steps show you how to articulate your desires clearly and how to navigate the tough asks lucratively. The Five Steps work even when you are experiencing self-doubt or are duking it out between your wants and desires and the wants and desires of others. These Five Steps will help you put your "game plan" together and rehearse for the tough conversations. Winging it won't work when it comes to asking for what you want. Wielding your wand and properly casting your spells works wonders if you know how to work it. Once you do, you'll be more adept at identifying all your yearnings from the surface cravings you have to the deeper longings that drive your life choices. It begins with knowing what you want in the first place.

CLARIFY YOUR REAL WANT

Years ago I worked for an executive who owned a vacation home on the southern coast of Spain. He was sure his summer home would bring him great joy. Despite being divorced, having a daughter that barely spoke to him, and employing a personal chef who preferred the company of a charcuterie board to that of his boss, off we all sojourned to enjoy the sunshine. Joining our merry band were the company's COO and CFO, as we were going away for the leadership team's annual strategic off-site. No sooner did we arrive than my boss decided that the new house needed a kayak. He wanted to get it delivered immediately so we could get out on the water. He ranted and raved over the phone for hours in broken Spanish, and by late afternoon the following day a kayak was delivered. It was at the dock no more than an hour when we watched two young kids climb down to the lake from the other side of the mountain, swim across, and steal the kayak in broad daylight. We literally watched them get away with it. My boss was livid. Jumping up and down and screaming across the ravine, he demanded they stop carrying away property that did not belong to them. I do not speak Spanish, but I do speak middle finger. I looked at the chef, who winked at me, and nodded back.

Two hours later, this same executive decided that if we went clubbing that night we would have a marvelous, youth-invigorating evening out with the "hip youngsters." I wanted a good night's sleep, but I also wanted to see the town. A quick siesta and two espressos later, I was game. Five resident employees showed up to join us at the local club at eleven o'clock that night. We were the only ones there. We drank our margaritas and attempted small talk in one another's native tongue before we all grew silent. "It's this club," the executive bellowed after his second drink. "Let's go to a better club. This one is terrible."

Well now that you've insulted the owners, yes, we should go, I thought. As it was thirty minutes before midnight, we joined the lonely bartender at the next club, who was still setting out glasses and getting his liquors in order. My boss ordered several rounds of tequila shots, and, as I'm a one-drink wonder, I offered mine to my younger colleagues, who were thrilled to get an extra boost for their nightly adventures, which would start *hours* later. Bored with canned music and no nightlife except for the bodies he forced into action, our executive called it quits. He loudly announced, "This is no fun!" The following day he was at it again at breakfast, with, "I'm going to buy another kayak. We must kayak."

"Must we?" I interjected. "What if we just relaxed? What if we walk through town, buy some fresh fish for tonight, have our strategy meeting, and relax on the patio this evening?" The chef nodded his head like a bobble doll. This executive was not so easily convinced.

"No water sports?" he asked.

"Next time," I reassured him. "Today, let's chill."

At around ten o'clock that night, when our sun-kissed hands helped themselves to a dessert tray of cheeses and fresh figs and our brains were still abuzz from all the innovative ideas we discussed in our meeting, the executive declared, "I told you this place was magical. Didn't I tell you this place was magical?!" His chef looked over at me and winked. I nodded again and tucked my wand a little lower in my pocket.

This executive didn't really want or need a kayak. He didn't really want or need to go clubbing. What he wanted was the fellowship of family and friends since he had lost the former and had a hard time with the latter. He wanted to know that, despite his personal transgressions, there were people who would show up and support him. He wanted people who cared about his business as much as he did. What he longed for most was to be accepted and respected—longings no kayak or nightclub could fulfill, but greater self-awareness about his deepest desires might deliver if he had taken time for self-reflection.

Fully grasping your underlying need will give you clarity about what is worth holding on to and what is not. It will help you focus your energy on purposeful actions to create a life of pleasure and purpose. When you hold on to what you want most and let go of the rest, you'll be amazed at how taking your own insightful dive pays off by delivering what you deeply want.

SATIATING YOUR DEEPER CRAVINGS

Not knowing what you want is a big barrier to getting what you really *do* want. You cannot articulate a clear ask in any conversation if you possess an unclear desire, and you will not satisfy your deepest cravings if you don't know what longings you're sincerely attempting to satiate.

First, to want is to be human. We all want things. Your cravings might be quirkily unique or pretty pedestrian, but every single day of your life you will want something.

Some days your wants will be tangible and materialistic. Other days you'll want to feel a certain way. Some of your wants will be enduring, others ephemeral. You might long for a good marriage, a good belly laugh, or just a good ole drool-inducing nap. You might desire emotional connection, intellectual stimulation, or a glass of old-vine zin.

Second, you spend much of your life expending energy on getting what you want. From educational degrees, jobs, and careers to relationships, kids, hobbies, and saving money for retirement. This doesn't even account for all the energy you expend on getting (or attempting to get) sex. You can't even stop your wanting post death. As a responsible, loving adult in today's complex society, you write your will and trust and get all of your affairs in order. You ensure certain individuals or institutions get precisely what you want them to get and your ridiculously selfish cousin doesn't sneak off with all of your treasured family heirlooms.

Maybe you're thinking, *I'm more of a low-maintenance Wanter.* You simply want to work less and relax more. Or maybe you want to make more money while you're working less and relaxing more. Whoa, wait, what you really want is to make more, work less, chillax a lot, have crazy-hot sex all the time, and fit into your pants from high school (or college—no need for extra pressure). Maybe, just maybe, you're completely nuts and want to never pick up dog poop or pay taxes ever again. Actually, you're not nuts, just normal. All of these desires are totally understandable and make complete sense. They just happen to compete with your other desires, which is why not getting clear on what you really, really—no, I'm serious—what you truly want is one of the biggest barriers to getting it. But cheer up because being aware of all these big barriers and knowing the steps to break through them is pretty magical. Grab your wand.

Imagine if I were to repeatedly ask you, "What do you want?"

You might start thinking, *I want a really successful career.*

Fair enough, but warning: this amazingly stellar career will require you to pay some taxes. "What else do you want?"

Dogs! I love dogs.

Well, you'll need a pooper-scooper. "What do you want next?"

Dessert! I love gelato. And cake.

News flash. A lot of gelato and cake were what made the button on your pants pop off. "What else?"

I want more exciting and exotic vacations that don't break the bank.

Certainly, totally get it, but I must mention, exciting and exotic does not always equate with cheap unless you define exciting and exotic as sleeping with foreigners in youth hostels.

Hmmm. Suddenly, you're a little less low-maintenance than you thought. It's easier to see, though, why getting what you want can be tricky. You often have competing commitments.

COMPETING COMMITMENTS

Competing commitments are one of the biggest barriers to getting what you want. You may want a promotion and more money, but you also want job security. When you think about stepping away from your current job to apply for a new one in a different state, or leaving corporate America altogether to start your own company, you feel this internal friction. This friction stems from your desire for autonomy and growth competing with your desire for certainty, comfort, and safety. One of the biggest human needs hardwired into your biology is your desire to avoid discomfort. Your brain knows today, just as well as your Neanderthal ancestor's brain knew thousands of years ago, you do not leave your current comfy cave for another without reducing your odds for failure. You must be certain that this next cave will be just as good or better, or that your backup cave at your cousin Lucy's has an extra bedroom, a warm fire, and plenty of beef jerky. You inherently know that before you roll up your fur, grab your club, and lug off to new adventures in a new cave on the far side of the valley, you'd better make a few phone calls first.

I once collaborated on a project with a creative agency. The woman who owned it knew all about competing commitments. In our very first conversation, she stated quite clearly, "There are three ingredients in every creative project we deliver. Fast. Creative. Cheap. I'd love to give you everything you want, but you'll only ever get two of the three. Fast and creative won't be cheap. Creative and cheap won't be fast. Fast and cheap will never be creative." This formula made it so much easier to figure out what we wanted most every single time.

One of the most common "competing commitments" that causes confusion is between feeling grateful and still wanting more. Feeling grateful and wanting more are often misinterpreted as competitors, when they are not. If you appreciate what you have and you're still longing for something different, it doesn't necessarily mean you're feeling ungrateful. It could be an indicator that you're unfulfilled. When you're feeling grateful, you'll notice and appreciate what *is* happening. When you're feeling ungrateful, you'll notice and be displeased about what is *not* happening. When you're feeling fulfilled, you'll experience pleasure in the life journey you're on and a sense of purpose that the life you are living is of significance. When you're feeling unfulfilled, you'll experience an absence of pleasure in the life journey you're on and a lack of purpose. It doesn't take away from the gratitude you can experience about your current blessings. Wanting to live a life of pleasure and purpose doesn't compete with your ability to notice and name your current blessings. Recognizing your longing to maximize your human journey will simply free you up to both appreciate your present existence and honor your desire to continue to create a life of even greater joy and meaning.

MARTY'S MIDLIFE MUDDLE

Marty was not exactly feeling or being his best self. His patience was shorter lately, he was frustrated with his colleagues and snapping more at his kids. He wouldn't call it a midlife crisis, per se. More like an awakening. A part of him was filled with gratitude. Things were going fairly well. He'd actually gotten most of what he wanted in life so far. A part of him was simply wondering how he might get more. He had a few minor questions that had been nagging him lately: *What do I want to do with my life? What legacy might I leave if I took a risk or two? What do I really believe? How did I end up here? Who am I? What do I really want?* You know, the lighthearted questions. A part of him was feeling good, and a part of him was feeling unmoored, a little lost. He wanted to have a more significantly meaningful impact over the next ten years but wondered if he was being too silly, too selfish. He began to wonder if he should just stop asking himself these frustrating questions. It would be so much easier if he could just stay on course, but even thinking about accepting the status quo brought up a restless energy inside him.

Every morning for the last three weeks, Marty had woken up tempted to make some quick surface change in his life. Even though he was ready to say goodbye to one phase of his life, he wasn't entirely sure how to create the next one. He thought about buying a new car, and no, he wasn't looking at minivans. He considered coloring his hair, wondering if a little less gray might be a good thing. He walked through a hip new clothing store for men but was pretty sure a wardrobe change wouldn't work. None of these young men had hips or waists or any muscle mass. *Who makes a store with only three sizes?* he snarled. Notwithstanding what he'd been preaching to his kids for years, he privately ruminated about punching a hole somewhere on his body or getting some ink. A tattoo might be just what he needed to rebel against his old way of life. In some physical, tangible way, he craved doing something that he could point to and say, *See, I'm changing! I'm not the same person I was yesterday.* Depending on the day and his alternating comfort level with risk, he'd considered everything from moving to a new city darn near overnight to simply rearranging his spice rack. *Ha! My spices are no longer arranged in alphabetical order but by cuisine type! I'm a creative genius in this next chapter of my life.*

Oh, you wild badass, Marty, don't get too carried away or you might start wearing your Friday underwear on Tuesdays, and who knows what crazy things will follow. More seriously, it is completely normal for Marty, for you (for everyone) to go through phases in your life. Refusing to recognize you are changing, and refusing to act meaningfully upon a new phase, is going to get you into trouble. Telling yourself that you are satisfied with the "same old, same old" is not going to cut it psychologically. Telling yourself you are just going through a phase (or that you will outgrow it) is not going to cut it. Marty clearly needed something deeper in his life besides a rearranged spice rack, but he was avoiding the tough conversation that would actually get it. Marty was the biggest obstacle preventing him from creating the life he so very much desired.

SCUBA CERTIFIED

When you force a surface want to materialize and it still leaves you longing for more, it's most likely a mask for what you really long for in your heart of hearts. Diving beneath the surface of your want to take a reflective and candid look at your deepest longings will keep you focused on giving yourself what you sincerely desire most. You think you want a certain something-something. You work your derriere off to get it. Voilà! You are now the proud owner of exactly what you wanted. Hmmm, now what? Getting what you wanted the way you thought you wanted it is turning out to be a big bummer. Oh, quick! Maybe if you hurl yourself down this other slippery slope you'll feel better. Nope? Oooh! Then try this false path! On and on it goes. Your collection of shoes, cars, marriages, degrees, startups, passport stamps, or whatever your obsession is continues to mask what it is you truly want.

Diving deep and having an honest dialogue with yourself helps you stay open to *how* your strongest wants might best be granted. When you lighten up and let go of controlling every detail, you can shift from desperate craving to living fully in the present and staying open to possibility. You might want to start your own bakery and sell the best cookies, cakes, and confections the world has ever tasted. You take out a loan, you work morning, noon, and night. Several months later, you're still weeks away from opening your doors to the public and you can't believe how many expletives fly out of your mouth on a daily basis. You realize this "owning your own business thing" is sucking the marzipan out of your bones. All you really wanted was to bake. Good grief. It's possible you didn't really want to turn your hobby into a vocation. You're now craving a vacation to think about how you might stop destroying your love for all things butter and cream. Note to self—it's not about avoiding the hard work or being lazy. Quite the contrary: if opening a bakery or an entire global chain of them is your deepest longing, you'll make it happen. It will require blood, sweat, tears, and the occasional curse word, but you'll love it. You'll get pleasure from the journey and mini-wins along the way, and it will be significantly meaningful to you. That's the difference. You'll feel fulfilled in the process, like a well-stuffed cream puff.

Surface wants can be dangerous traps in your personal life too. Singles are frequently told to make a list of criteria they are looking for in an ideal soulmate. This can doom a romantic relationship from the start if you find someone that meets all of your surface criteria but fulfills little to none of your deepest requirements. Suppose you make a long list of criteria that your picture-perfect partner will possess. With thick inventory in hand, including hair color, height measurements, and a love for all things beaches and mountains, you're so busy waiting for Mr. or Ms. "Perfect Person" you miss out on the truly "Amazing Person for You." Oh, I know, this incredibly gorgeous specimen may one day stand before you on your screen and seem so perfect you can't help but swipe right. So tall. So dark. So stunning. But tall, dark, and stunning on the surface may turn out to be tall, dark, and totally not your "deepest-longing type" in real life. Why? Because at the end of the day, what you really want goes beyond some visual fantasy on a picture-perfect photoshopped magazine cover or dating app. What you want is a partner who gets you, laughs with you, emotionally connects with you, knows what to say when you're feeling stressed out, and knows precisely where to touch you to send your body into orbit. Now there's your celestial soulmate.

Getting what you really want, at your deepest core, requires taking a magnifying glass and holding it up to yourself. Out of the sun, of course, so you don't burn a hole in your skull. Although that's metaphorically what you're doing: you're drilling into yourself to get a better look at what's really going on inside of you. There's no way on Earth (or any planet) you're going to get what you really want if you start pursuing the wrong things for the wrong reasons.

LET GO OF THE HOW

Be open to the notion that what you want wants you too; it may just take an unexpected form. Believing there are multiple ways to get what you want creates options, and when you have options, you exponentially increase the chances of getting what you want. Whether you want to make more money, have more job autonomy, travel more, spend more time with family, or just sit down and watch the game in peace, there's more than one way to make it happen.

Matt wanted kids for years. What he didn't know was that he was going to end up marrying a woman with two of her own children and they would adopt a baby together. Only then did he finally feel fulfilled.

Kate majored in English. She wanted to write a novel. After years of strife and stress and still no completed manuscript, she started her own blogging site. Today, she reaches thousands of readers who engage with her weekly. Now she feels fulfilled.

Alan spent most of his career proving to others he was a smart, successful business owner. If you weren't sure if he was truly a brilliant entrepreneur, you could just look at his McMansion or fleet of sports cars as proof. Yet none of these things were satisfying Alan's strongest cravings.

Getting what you want isn't always going to mean you get to control the whole *how*, nor do you necessarily want to. Gripping the reins so tight that there's only one way for your want to manifest can prevent potentially awesome things from happening. Being flexible and creative about your want list is key. From time to time, you'll get what you want in unexpected ways. Sometimes these unpredictable ways are better than you anticipated. Excellent news! If you force your want to happen in a very specific manner, sometimes you won't get it at all or, worse, you'll get it, but it will leave you empty and unfulfilled and wanting the exact opposite.

With any deep desire, hang on to it tightly, but let go of what it ultimately looks like in the real world. Matt wanted kids and got them, but not in the way that he thought he would. Kate wanted to write a novel and didn't get it. She got something better. What Matt and Kate both wanted was deeper than their surface want. Matt's true longing was to be a dad. The kids didn't need to biologically be his. Kate wanted to write and have her work resonate with readers; it didn't need to be through a novel. If Matt had insisted there was only one way to get what he wanted, he may never have gotten it. If Kate had insisted that she could only express herself through a novel, she would never have experienced the rewarding feelings she received from interacting with her readers in real time and knowing her writing was having an immediate impact.

Alan, on the other hand, was acquiring lots and lots of stuff, but it wasn't what he really wanted. Oh sure, it was fun to drive a new car for a week or two, but what disarmed him was how quickly the feelings of excitement dissipated and he found himself unhappy again. Hence the next new toy. Alan was forcing *how* he was going to be happy because he hadn't figured out that happiness wasn't the real driver behind his purchases. Alan was afraid to take a deep dive and look at his own vulnerable yearnings. Sadly, his unwillingness to dive deep and learn about his innermost wants was preventing him from getting exactly what he craved most: to feel worthy and included. No car could take Alan to a destination he wasn't even aware he longed to visit.

OPTIONS KEEP YOU SANE

Too often, you think there's only one way to get what you want. For those of you that do begin to see possibility, you often take a small step into the two-option *or* stage. You start thinking your want can only be satisfied in two ways. It can either be satisfied with this choice *or* that choice. It can be fulfilled if you go this way *or* that way. You can have Option A *or* Option B. This type of thinking limits possibilities. Rather than truncating possibility, you can vastly expand your options when you start thinking, *How else?* or *What else?* How fun would it be to say, *How else might I get this* and *this* and *this? What am I missing?* Letting go of the *how* and opening up to a wide range of alternatives tips the scale in favor of you getting what you want.

For example, Derek was frequently praised by his colleagues for not micromanaging them. He inherently believed he had hired a talented team, and he trusted them to use their skills to make things happen. At the beginning of each year, he would lay out an outline of his strategic and operational goals for his division. He then requested that everyone on his team add their passion and expertise to ensure their buy-in and commitment to making the goals happen. He would ask himself, *What am I missing?* and then ask his direct reports, *How might you personally make it better?* These types of questions are powerful motivators. While he definitely had a vision and checked in on their progress along the way, *how* each person on the team decided to go about their task was a personal choice. He also knew if he invited open-ended contributions, the end result would exceed his expectations. What he wanted most was to meet and exceed the goals while everybody was having fun and felt good about their individual contribution.

Lisa wanted to make more money. She and her husband were living paycheck to paycheck and they both wished they could afford to take a vacation. Lisa asked her boss for a raise and the boss said no. Lisa went to HR and was told a salary freeze was in effect. Instead of thinking she was out of options and should give up, Lisa let go of the idea that more money had to be in the form of a raise. Two days after she opened up to the idea that money could come from different sources, her friend called and asked her if she might help out with an event over the weekend. The catering company Lisa's friend worked for was short a staff member. It would pay $300 for the night. Lisa was thrilled at the prospect of earning more money and accepted the offer to work. Filled with hope and the knowledge that she could get what she wanted if she stayed open to possibilities, Lisa decided to schedule a vacay-planning date with her husband. The following Friday night, she served up homemade piña coladas while she and her husband put a budget together. A few minutes into the process, her husband said, "Planning a vacation while drinking piña coladas makes me feel like we're a little bit on vacation already."

Staying open to *possibility* not only creates unexpected moments of joy but it may also allow for a highly anticipated want to manifest in a very unanticipated way.

LAW OF RECIPROCITY

When you think about what it is you want, it's vital to think about all parties involved and their wants too. Ignoring the Law of Reciprocity will almost guarantee that you don't get what you want or that it will take a heck of a lot longer. Wanting is not in and of itself bad. Wanting to the exclusion of anyone else's wants is selfish. In terms of dandelions, do not be weedy. Taking the time to uncover all the facets of your wants and someone else's wants, both on the surface and underneath, helps you create more space for possibilities and alternative options for *how* your want can manifest. Delving into the other person's wants can help you help yourself. Meaning when you honor another's desires and wants and work toward fulfilling them first or simultaneously with yours, you are drastically increasing the odds of getting what you want.

A quick, effective technique for encouraging reciprocity from another is to label your action a "partnership pact." When someone thanks you for your help, instead of simply saying, "You're welcome" or, even worse, "No problem," say one of the following lines, depending on the nature of your relationship with the other person.

- It's what teammates do for one another.
- It's what friends do for one another.
- It's what business partners do for one another.
- It's what couples do for one another.
- It's what brothers (or sisters) do for one another.

These "partnership pacts" reinforce that helping one another to get what you each want is how you play the game and both win.

WHERE YOU MIGHT GET STUCK

A word of caution: when it comes to articulating your wants, vague language will yield vague results. If your ask is not specific, you will not get what you really want.

I want my kids to be happy.

Awesome. You've spawned kids that are so happy that by age fifteen they're totally irresponsible and carefree.

Can I amend my ask?! you plead. *I guess what I really want is for them to be responsible and safe, get good grades, and feel included in their high school community.*

I want to be married.

Five years into your relationship, all you want is to take your left-hand ring and turn it into a right-wrist bracelet.

Can I amend my ask?! you plead. *I want someone who doesn't lie and sneak around.*

I want thirty grand to manifest in my life.

Out of nowhere, an unexpected tax notice shows up in the mail. The Internal Revenue Service claims you filed improperly and paid too few taxes seven years ago. You owe so much in back taxes and interest that it adds up to—wait, you guessed it—thirty grand.

Can I amend my ask?! you plead. *This is not magical. This stinks.*

I want to live abroad. Wait, who said anything about Siberia? Can I amend my ask?! you plead. *I was envisioning learning the language of love with a baguette tucked under my arm.*

What a sloppy way to use your wand. Get particular. Precision is the point, my petunias, and then—and no, I'm not crazy when I now say—let go of the *how*. Do not get picky about the *how*; get detailed about your deeper want. Then ask for that yearning and watch *how* the magic unfolds.

Here's the difference between fuzzy and a fine amount of finicky while still letting go of the how.

Fuzzy want: *I want my kids to be happy.*

Finer-tuned want: *I want my kids to grow up to be responsible, healthy, and happy adults who contribute to society in a way that brings them pleasure and purpose.*

(Nobody said anything about forcing them into the family business.)

Fuzzy want: *I want to be married.*

Finer-tuned want: *I want to be in a committed, respectful, loving, passionate, fun relationship.*

(Nobody but Beyoncé said anything about putting a ring on it. Or that it has to be a certain Luke, Laura, or Sam. Just be certain that you're asking for an amazing match for yourself.)

Fuzzy want: *I'm manifesting thirty grand into my life.*

Finer-tuned want: *I want a healthy relationship with money. I want money to be a positive energy in my life. I want to create opportunities for money to flow into my life in unexpectedly abundant ways. PS: And right now I could use an extra thirty grand to pay Uncle Sam.*

(Nobody said to let this request dangle. If you've got a rich aunt, off with you now. Go ask her. If you've got a brilliant idea, off with you to the patent office.)

Fuzzy want: *I want to live abroad.*

Finer-tuned want: *I want to experience other cultures, make friends with people from faraway places, eat amazing food from around the globe, and not get dysentery, malaria, or Montezuma's revenge along the way.*

(Nobody said you couldn't have fantabulous adventures. You've just gotta get your shots, take your pills, not drink the water, and be open to multiple countries.)

A MAGICAL PHRASE FOR STEP 1: *HOW MIGHT WE...?*

With your clarified outcome (i.e., your want) in hand, it's time to use your first magical phrase to flip any want into a brilliant ask. These three small but mighty words are the crown jewel of magical spells. Your business and life without these three words is like life without sunshine (i.e., you're in the dark, the very, very dark).

Without learning how to wield your wand with the power of *How might we...?* your world is a wild wilderness. You're without a compass and you have little to no navigational skills, but you still hear well. And there are lots of scary noises. Well, that just sucks. But...it doesn't have to be so dark. Or so scary. There's a brilliant way to unsuck it. Starting with the magical phrase *How might we...?*

Placing the words *How might we...?* at the beginning of your stated desire, so you turn it into a question, will raise the quality of your thinking instantly and have you (and others) working toward your want, pronto.

These three magical and mighty words set the tone for a highly profitable conversation.

How might we...instantly conveys that you expect everyone to do some thinking.

How might we...instantly invites the collective sharing of ideas.

How might we...instantly requests engagement and participation.

How might we...instantly expresses inclusion and collaboration.

How might we...instantly triggers the brain to start thinking.

This is not *me*, this is *we*. This is not low-level data-dumping or whining or venting; this is open-ended problem-solving about getting what "we" want.

Maybe you want to:

- Increase sales by 12 percent
- Adopt a baby
- Ensure the acquisition goes smoothly
- Launch a wildly successful sales campaign
- Complete Phase One on time and, better yet, under budget
- Expand your brand

- Get your kids to put down their phones and engage
- Raise money for a charity or cause
- Create a healthier company culture
- Improve your marriage
- Create a safer world for your kids

Unfortunately, when you first write down your want as a statement, your brain's initial reaction is going to be *That's nice. Yep, I want that too. Jolly great goal.* But it doesn't do anything. Your brain is not triggered to think, to take action, to figure out *how* to get inspired to achieve it. This inaction stems from the fact that the brain needs a bigger trigger. To effectively wake up your brain and ignite your thinking, you must flip your objective from a statement to a question using *How might we...?*

These are the three most brilliant words for igniting thinking in your own brain and all the brains of your colleagues, direct reports, team members, supervisors, board members, and family members. These three words fire up your neurons and kick-start engagement, problem-solving, and action-taking.

- How might we increase sales by 12 percent?
- How might we adopt a baby?
- How might we ensure the acquisition goes smoothly?
- How might we launch a wildly successful sales campaign?

- How might we complete Phase One on time and, better yet, under budget?
- How might we expand my brand?
- How might we get our kids to put down their phones and engage?
- How might we raise money for a charity or cause?
- How might we create a healthier company culture?
- How might we improve our marriage?
- How might we create a safer world for our kids?

Posed as a question, your brain is immediately engaged in figuring out how to answer and fulfill this want of yours. You start reflecting on past successes and failures. You start evaluating current conditions, variables, and options. You start predicting exactly *how* you and your posse might best move forward and make it happen.

THE POWER OF POSITIVITY

If you're not kidding around and you really want what you say you want, it's imperative to write positive and future oriented *How might we...* questions. Positivity is not kumbaya; it's neuroscience. We know from fMRI (functional magnetic resonance imaging) machines that when we ask someone a negative or backward-focused question, they get defensive and their brain's prefrontal cortex neural activity decreases. What does increase is their desire to fight, flee, or play the lame blame-game.

Why did you do that? Why can't you sell more? Why does our company culture stink? These types of questions generate defensive reactions and potential expletives.

Boss: Minion, why can't you just do your job?

Minion: Uh, because we're working in a toxic culture with a tyrant of a boss who tells us we're stupid and forces us to defend ourselves all the time.

Backward-focused questions lead to less ideation, less problem-solving, less collaboration. The cost is tangible and exponential. Alternatively, when you write a *How might we...* question that is optimistic and forward-looking, the brain lights up. It gets excited about creating a better future, solving the problem, getting over the hurdle, or fixing what's broken. It gets eager to find a solution to propel everyone in a better direction to get whatever it is you're after.

Example:

Suppose your original objective is *I want to increase sales by 12 percent.*

Begin with brainstorming several possible *How might we...* questions for your objective until you get the one you deem best.

Possible *How might we...* questions:

- How might we increase sales by 12 percent?
- How might we upsell our current customer base to increase sales by 12 percent?
- How might we meet and exceed 12 percent sales growth?
- How might we ideally leverage our best-selling products to meet and exceed 12 percent sales growth?
- How might we focus on our new product launch to meet and exceed 12 percent sales growth?
- How might we best define three ideal revenue streams to meet and exceed 12 percent sales growth?

A bonus byproduct of positively brainstorming your initial *How might we...* question is that it yields clarity about what you and others *specifically* need to address and *how* you might all best solve it. Once you finalize your initial *How might we...* question it will drive and guide your conversations.

When you have an individual objective, such as *I want to lose weight, I want to get my finances in order*, or *I want to learn to play the cello*, phrasing the objective as a *How might I...* question is the best way to start.

- How might I best lose weight?
- How might I get my finances in order?

How might I start learning to play the cello?

Then immediately ask, *Who might I ask to help me?*

This question appropriately reminds you that you don't have to tackle this challenge on your own. There will be others willing to help you as long as you ask. Once others are on board, switch back to *we.* Your *How might we...* is the big question that overarchingly states that this conversation is about a bigger, "badder," better, bolder, brighter future...that we are going to co-create together so we can all get whatever we want.

SETTING HIMSELF UP FOR SUCCESS

Kirk wanted a promotion. On the surface, it seemed pretty straightforward. However, when he began thinking through the questions *What do I really want? How do I want to feel now and down the road? What are the underlying drivers/needs behind my desire for a promotion?* and *What's the full outcome I seek both short-term and long-term?* he realized his desire for a promotion went deeper than his surface aspiration. He also wanted more responsibility. He was getting bored and needed more intellectual stimulation. His current projects were a little lackluster, and he preferred to feel more energized and engaged by his work. He also knew that while he absolutely wanted more money, it was sincerely a secondary want. What he wanted more was for this next move to put him on track to be a member of a high-level creative team in a few years. Kirk recognized he was willing to take a lateral move at first if it meant getting to use more of his creative talent, but there would also need to be a promotion within the next six months. The more he thought it through, the more clarity he got around the best game plan to put in motion. When he unpacked any possible competing commitments he had that might prevent him from pursuing a promotion wholeheartedly, he acknowledged that he did not want to be away from his family any more than he was currently. All this insight led to greater clarity for honing his want.

Kirk then practiced reciprocity with respect to his boss's possible needs. He asked himself a few questions about her possible wants, such as *What might she want? How might she want to feel? What might be her underlying drivers?* and *What's the long-term play she's possibly after?* The answers to these questions helped him peel back a few layers and better prepare for his upcoming conversation with her. He was fairly certain she wouldn't be threatened by his request. Quite the contrary, it might be more of an issue that she wouldn't want to lose him. Kirk knew he was already doing a lot of the heavy lifting, including covering for a dude out on family leave. From this perspective, his boss might feel anxious about his request. She'd need to know he was committed to seeing all of his current projects through to successful completion. She might also feel better knowing that his first goal was about upping his responsibilities and getting creatively stimulated rather than gunning for a new title.

With all of these wants in mind, Kirk knew that his opening words needed to set the right tone and tenor from the start. He wanted to keep the conversation positive and forward-focused. He decided that a thoughtful way to start the conversation might be with the question *How might we create a game plan so I can become an even more integrated, successful team player?* This overarching question encouraged an open dialogue with lots of possible win-win scenarios, including, but not limited to, a promotion. By letting go of the *how* while hanging on to his needs, Kirk knew there'd be more than one way to get what he wanted.

Even though Kirk was feeling a little bored with his current situation, he didn't want to show up to his boss's office with lifeless energy. In fact, if he was ever going to expand his responsibilities, he needed to demonstrate to his boss that his positive energy could not be contained. With a positive framework established from the very start of the conversation, he mapped out a conversational flow that included the stellar progress of his current projects and all the things that were working for him as an individual and for the team as a whole. From a foundation of strengths, he would then address his objectives for the next ninety days and the benefits to everyone when they were reached and possibly exceeded.

Only then did Kirk plan on expressing his concerns about how he was not being stimulated to the level he desired. He knew it would be important at this juncture in the conversation to separate out his present successes from future opportunities. Reminding his boss that he was currently a dedicated high performer would serve as a springboard for where his talent and dedication could best serve next. His last move would be to focus on how he might get more creatively challenged as he shared his willingness to take on more responsibilities. This thoughtful flow, centered around everyone's wants, would keep both Kirk and his boss moving in the direction of their desires.

Kirk's conversation outline:

How might we create a game plan so I can become an even more integrated, successful team player?

- What are the strengths of our current projects (people, processes, etc.)?
- What's currently working for us, individually and as a team?
- How might we best stay aligned on these current projects for the next ninety days?

- What's the benefit/payoff to each of us, the team, and the company when these projects are successfully completed?
- What are our concerns as we move forward?
- How might I begin to get more intellectual and creative stimulation going forward?
- How might I ideally expand my responsibilities and impact in the next twelve months?
- How might we best move forward toward our goals? What's the first and best next step?

Kirk knowing precisely what he wanted was his best first step to getting it.

GET WHAT YOU WANT: WHAT YOU SO DEEPLY WANT

Take a moment to write down one of your most coveted wants or most prioritized objectives. Similar to the examples above, it could be a personal want of yours, a team or group objective at work, or a goal you share with your spouse or a friend. Be bold. Be brave. Pick a want with gravitas. You might want to leverage an opportunity, solve a challenge, navigate a change, maximize an initiative, or cross a particular finish line. Pick something that truly matters to you.

I want ....

Before you begin any critical conversation, consider your short-term and long-term goals so you gain perspective on the full scope of what you're seeking. You don't have to choose a finite point in time, such as an outcome exactly nine months down the road (unless this conversation is about making a baby), but absolutely think about the big picture. Consider what you want out of *this* upcoming conversation and how it will play out down the road. The following questions will help you gain clarity about what you're really after so that you can articulate it more easily and be more open to how it might best manifest.

- What do I really want? That is, what will the above want get me (short-term and/or long-term)?

....

....

- How do I want to feel (short-term and long-term)?

....

....

- What are the underlying drivers/needs behind my surface want? (Dive deeper.)

....

....

- What's the full outcome I seek? (Hone it—fine-tune it.)

....

....

If you're not the only person participating in this conversation (as in, it's not a conversation with yourself), answer the following questions as well.

- What might the other person(s) want (short-term and/or long term)?

....

....

- How might they want to feel (short-term and long-term)?

....

....

What might be the underlying drivers/needs behind their wants? (Dive deeper.)

....

....

What's the full outcome they might seek? (Hone it— fine-tune it to the best of your ability, or ask 'em.)

....

....

When you clarify your wants and incorporate another person's wants into your vision, you'll foster alignment and increase engagement. Taking the time to sincerely acknowledge another's feelings demonstrates empathy. Staying positive and forward-focused influences everyone's energy and actions toward co-creating a future you all desire. The best way to start framing the upcoming conversation is to turn the wants into an inclusive *How might we...* question. It can set up the entire framing and flow for where you want to take it.

How might we...

....

Working through the flow of the conversation ahead of time helps you maintain momentum and prevents the scenario of you taking two steps forward and then three steps back. To establish a profitable flow, consider the following:

How do I want to start the conversation?

....

....

....

What tone and tenor do I first wish to convey?

....

....

....

What two to three main ideas, concepts, or examples do I wish to share?

....

....

....

💬 What's the best order in which to share them?

....

....

....

💬 What outline of questions might create the best flow throughout the conversation?

....

....

....

💬 How do I want to close?

....

....

....

Knowing precisely what you want is the best first step to getting the life *you* desire.

So, what happened to Marty, the gentleman I described earlier in this step as being in a midlife muddle? I know Marty well. I coached him for several months. What Marty wanted first and foremost, deep down, was a more intimate and satisfying relationship with his wife. After thirty years of "settling for mediocrity and feeling inadequate," Marty led some tough conversations with his wife. And they worked it out. Awesomely so. Marty now has more sex than he ever imagined possible, and he finally feels like he and his wife are in sync. Marty no longer needs my coaching, but he has referred several of his unhappy friends my way. That's how powerful each step is in getting you closer to what you want. Marty turned his relationship around and got a best friend back with Step 1, and it was Step 2 that changed his life and marriage (and his sex life) forever. If you're implementing all the tools in Step 1 and you're ready to kick it into overdrive, now it's time to ask yourself if you are seeking connection or power. The two seldom go together, as you will see in Step 2.

SEEK CONNECTION OR POWER—RARELY BOTH

On a scale of one to ten, how awkward was this moment? A few years ago a friend and I were sitting on the living room couch talking with a married couple he knew from ages past. It had been several years since they'd all gathered together, and, as it was my initial introduction to them, we were innocently exchanging pleasantries and sipping iced tea. Suddenly, the conversation took an unexpected turn. The wife patted my knee and asked, "Don't you think you should be able to follow your dreams?"

As an optimistic, dream-pursuing kinda gal, I nodded enthusiastically in agreement. "Sure!"

"And don't you think if that dream involves teaching the word of God it should be extra sacred?"

"Sure," I responded, eyeing a bug doing the backstroke in my glass. *Whatever floats your boat*, I thought, *and this little dude is in serious need of a paddle.*

"And don't you think no one should have the right to take your dreams away?" she implored, raising her voice an octave while managing the loudest stage whisper I'd heard since my theater days in college. My spidey sense kicked in just as the bug in my glass got caught under a shifting cube. He was going down.

"Sure?" I questioned, looking up at her.

"And if someone has a husband who can't keep a job, can't even find a job, do you think that should mean she should give up her dream job of sharing the word of God with young adults?"

Ummmm. Uh. D'oh! While I was no longer sure about any of this conversation, I was dang sure the bug in my glass was not the only thing drowning in the room that afternoon.

She continued, "I know, I know, I'm the one with the MBA, I'm the one with the advanced degree, but does that mean I have to be the sole provider and give up my dreams? We're talking about the love of Christ!"

It was precisely at that moment that I looked over and

noted her husband and my friend had stopped talking. The look on her husband's face shifted, almost imperceptibly, but not before I witnessed his vulnerability and pain. In an instant, his emasculated, disrespected identity and his own raw self-loathing peeked out from behind a mask of stoicism. All of it was quickly pushed aside and repressed when he asked, "You guys following the Olympics?" A passive-aggressive power play had been won, but their connection was lost.

POWER PLAYS ARE TERRIBLE PLAYDATES

Where does a series of events begin? At home, it may start with the dishwasher or, more specifically, the incorrect loading of it. It could conceivably be the high electric bill and all the lights you turn off every single frickin' night before you crawl into bed, or why your spouse insists on spending Thanksgiving with their family every year. Or perchance your arguments start more innocuously, with how the towels were folded and put away (or not) or which way the toilet paper hangs—under or over—or why this person that you "love dearly" does everything wrong. Of course, it's not wrong; it's just not how you want it.

Somewhere along the way, these seemingly harmless, unresolved disagreements lead to bigger, more consequential disagreements. These bigger conflicts, left unattended, will cultivate into raw open wounds, possibly passive-aggressive behaviors or worse, full-on battles intent on destruction. These imbalances of power and the subsequent power plays that result will end in a great deal of pain.

The only long-term relationships that thrive are the ones where both people crave *connection*. When you crave connection, you solve problems through communication and empathy. When you crave connection, you actively listen and seek understanding. The goal is to help your partner feel understood, accepted, and loved, and for them to know and truly believe they have a witness to their life. When you seek connection, ironically, you must acknowledge there is a separate sentient human being sitting across from you with his or her own wants and desires. Hence why you need to connect. They. Are. Separate. From. You. And. They. Are. Not. You. You must accept this fact before you can connect.

Seeking connection does not mean agreeing on everything, nor does it mean you won't argue on occasion. Seeking connection as a couple simply means that you stay open and curious about your partner and his or her needs and wants. It means you're still learning about your partner and you respect your partner, even when you disagree or approach an issue from different viewpoints. Respecting differences while constructively addressing conflicts will help your connection grow stronger. When your connection to another is stronger, you'll want to help them get what they want, and they'll want to help you get what you want. As if by magic, what they want *is* what you want (for them). I've coached couples who were members of different political parties. I've seen married newscasters express diametrically opposite views on television and not be mean or vindictive to each other or overtly disparage each other's views. This is possible only when there is mutual respect.

However, when one person craves *power* and the other person craves *connection*, the relationship eventually disintegrates and way too many wants go unfulfilled. If you're the one craving connection and your partner craves power, you'll quickly find it draining to give in to your partner's insecurities, ego trips, or self-centeredness. It's tiresome to take the high road all the time or be the one that must always apologize first. It can be taxing to take the initiative in smoothing things over, "giving in," or going along so as to get along and keep the peace. Frankly, it's downright exhausting when you're the only mature adult in the relationship. Therefore, the two logical options are to quit the relationship or change it.

When both people crave *power* (and stay in an unchanged relationship), they often destroy one another. When you are part of a two-person intimate power struggle, you solve problems by being "right," by winning, or both.

Often, being right or winning isn't even enough. Someone must be wrong in order for you to be right. Someone must lose. That same someone must also feel like they are "less than" in order for you to feel like you are "more than." In power plays, the wants and desires of others take a back seat to your wants and desires because, unquestionably, your desires matter more. Yikes! No wonder "power couples" often end up in couples' therapy.

PLAYING TO STRENGTHS

To be clear, having power in a personal relationship is not the same thing as *accepting assignment* for your areas of influence and responsibility within the partnership. Influencing by *accepting assignment* is about playing to our strengths so we may positively contribute. In your most intimate relationship, there are many areas of influence: from how much time you two spend together, to the activities that you participate in during this time, to managing commitments with family and friends, to raising kids. Other areas of influence may include religious commitments, household chores, careers, and your place of residence. When you seek connection, you are focused on understanding your partner's wants and desires, expressing your own wants and needs, and problem-solving together so that as many of your individual and collective desires can be met. You compromise, take turns, or find an equilibrium acceptable to you both.

Having a better understanding of where influence resides within your relationship will help you gain clarity as to why you are or are not getting what you want. Once you see where influence rests, you can discern if the energy resulting from it is positive or negative. If it is negative or simply imbalanced, you can then take action to share it more equitably. Perhaps you have more influence on your family's yearly budget with respect to both expenditures and investments. Your expertise and passion for mutual funds, stocks, and life insurance are greater than your partner's. You accept this assignment of caring for and managing the finances, but you do not use it as a power play over your partner. You do not belittle or criticize your partner's lack of knowledge, nor do you control the purse strings, and you make sure you and your partner make financial decisions together.

In some relationships, one partner might coordinate all the vacation activities, whereas in other relationships both parties want to plan together. Sometimes both individuals in a couple get excited by the same types of adventures, while some couples and families alternate activity choices to ensure everyone gets to participate in something they enjoy. You might be the one who wants to do all the vacation research, or you might be the type who wants to simply show up and toast to the adventures ahead, knowing you'll pick up the slack in another area of influence.

When you crave connection, you accept assignment for contributing positively. When you crave power, you're grasping onto assignment for control, and you use your power to manipulate, dominate, and hurt in order to feed your ego. You believe it's the only way to ensure you get what you want. Sadly, it may get you what you want on the surface or in the short term, but at what sacrifice? Oh yes, there may be fleeting feelings of victory, superiority, righteousness, and hierarchy, but then what? Most typically, you begin to feel worse. First, because what you really crave is still not satisfied. Second, because eventually your partner will no longer give a flying fig about your wants. Over time, your power antics lead to disrespect and distance. Over half of all marriages end in divorce. A base cause is that one or both partners seek power over the other. Seeking power or buttressing your ego are two surefire ways to not get what you want.

Power and influence are fascinating dynamics in all of your relationships. Choosing power or connection will impact how you resolve conflict, the degree to which you can persuade one another, how and when you share information, and, ultimately, how much you trust the other person and how safe you feel. In your most intimate personal relationship, when you consistently choose connection over power, your relationship will last. When your most personal relationship is healthy and functional, it gives you so much of what you desire and often more.

Before I go any further, there's certainly a flip side to using your power. Power can be used for good. Owning your power will help you assert yourself with colleagues, friends, family members, and even your partner when it comes to your nonnegotiable needs. Possible opportunities to appropriately express your power may include respecting differences, honoring schedules, accepting specific choices, and establishing boundaries.

As long as you realize that you're purposefully pulling a power play to protect yourself or rightfully expand your sense of self, then go for it. I mean, for crying out loud, how many times are you going to let so-and-so say such-and-such before *you* say something?! Just know that the overall best way to get whatever you want in your most intimate of relationships is to ask yourself, *Am I seeking connection or am I seeking power?* When both people prioritize connection, your relationship thrives. Which way the toilet paper hangs, how many lights are on, and where to spend Thanksgiving are all solvable problems for those seeking connection.

DISCONNECTED AND IT FEELS SO BAD

What if you're thinking, *But we're already disconnected. We're already worlds apart and saying snarky things, and this is not what I want, but I don't know how to turn it around.*

It's time to hit the reset button. I tell my clients all the time, "I'm not coaching your significant other. I'm coaching you." The only person who can guarantee that your words and actions will change in the next conversation is you. If future conversations with your spouse are going to shift toward connection and away from power, you need to be clear on the distinctive disconnections you are experiencing. Specifically, are you experiencing disconnection because you are feeling:

- Unloved
- Left out
- Unsafe
- Disrespected
- Unheard
- Ignored or dismissed
- Misunderstood
- Underutilized, like your gifts and talents aren't shining in the relationship
- Like one of your core needs or desires is not being met (Which one? How so?)

Once you've identified a specific disconnection or several, ask yourself:

- What do I want or need right now to feel restored?
- What needs to happen?
- What actions do I need to take to get what I want or need?

This is where you may need to "flip the flapjack" and use your personal power to assert your wants and needs. Keeping the connection in your relationship is *not* about keeping the peace to avoid abuse or neglect. In fact, I'm encouraging the opposite of compliance. Use your voice and take actions that express your commitment to creating the relationship you want.

If you can't take significant action steps immediately, give yourself some grace and figure out a small turtle step that will move you in a healthier direction. Reconnection happens when we get clarity around what we want and then take action to manifest it. Prioritizing connection leads to greater renewal and restoration. If you're not feeling certain about where to start with your spouse, simply say, "I love you. I love us when we're loving on each other. I want us to practice loving on each other more. I want us to focus on connecting." Then hand your bestie this section to read.

You are your most content self when you get the connectivity you seek. You feel less cranky, less anxious, more grounded, and more secure. When you experience these emotions more of the time, you feel restored, kinder, and more compassionate. Not in a people-pleasing way, but in a genuine, authentic, *Hey everybody, I'm feeling like a peaceful badass right now. I'm getting what I want, so let me help you get what you want* kinda way. It's such fun when you get more of whatever you want because it inspires you to help others get whatever they want. The momentum that gets generated is a two-way street—the more you give, the more you get.

WHERE YOU MIGHT GET STUCK

Sometimes the people who love you don't want you to get what you want because it conflicts with what they want. Your brother may not be 100 percent supportive of your desire to move because he still wants you as his built-in babysitter. Your parents may not want you to switch careers and pursue your passion for photography because they love telling their friends you're a successful scientist. Your spouse may not want you to go back to school because you currently cook almost every night and manage the household.

Switching the focus of a conversation away from the competing commitments and focusing on a commitment you share is the fastest way to create a connection and move toward getting what you want. You'll either create a joint resolution that's acceptable to you both or you will need to assert your personal power. Staying stuck in an argument about a surface want delays satisfaction for everyone, causes additional and unnecessary stress, and prevents connection. Sometimes asking a straightforward question such as the following can shift a tough conversation into a profitable one by resetting the point under discussion:

- Might we agree that we both want to live our best lives?
- Might we agree that we both want to be happy?
- Might we agree that we're both trying to use our best gifts and talents for good?
- Can we agree that we both want to feel fulfilled?
- Can we agree that we both want...?

With an aligned want you can then ask, "How might we best support one another in doing so?"

Other times, a scenario might be more complex. For example, perhaps you and your spouse are considering moving out of state for a new job opportunity. You are excited to go. It's a significant promotion for you, but your partner would prefer to stay. The kids are settled in school, your partner has an enjoyable job, and both sets of grandparents live close by. You and your spouse are weighing all of these options one night after the kids are in bed, when your partner mentions that both sets of grandparents are not happy about the possibility of increased distance between them and their grandchildren.

You're triggered by this comment. You've already been feeling guilty about taking the kids farther away from their grandparents, and now you're feeling slightly ganged up on too. Have they all been talking behind your back? You're wondering if your spouse betrayed your confidence, when your partner immediately responds with, "No, I didn't encourage their input. I can see by the look on your face that you're feeling bullied. It's not why I shared. They mentioned it, and I said we hadn't made our decision yet. I didn't invite their input, but I'm talking with you now. I have to say I like having them close by. It's good for the kids and it's good for me."

Without thinking, you react with, "Yeah, well, this promotion is good for *me*. It's exactly what I've been working for all these years."

Your spouse responds with, "Silly me, here I thought you were working for our family."

This type of exchange perpetuates angst and disconnection. Reacting defensively is understandable; however, it's not productive. Responding with a shared commitment shifts the conversation away from power and toward connection. Suppose your spouse has just shared the desire to stay. You replace your reaction above with the more considered response of "I hear you. It makes sense that you want to stay. A part of me wants to stay too. I'm torn. I'm feeling guilty about possibly moving the kids away, and I'm also excited about this opportunity.

I've worked really hard for it and the money is good. I'm seeing it boost the kids' college accounts. Might we set going or staying aside for a minute and talk about what we both really want long-term? I want to reset with what matters most to you, me, and us as a team."

Whether or not you go or stay will not matter as much down the road as making a decision that is inclusive, respectful, and loving. Staying and resenting your spouse won't be fun. Going and having a hostile partner is just as unpleasant. I won't sugarcoat it. These conversations are not easy. You may get upset; your spouse may lose it and need to apologize. Nonetheless, if you start with what you both value and want most and where your values and wants align, it makes it less painful to compromise. Instead of seeing the decision through the lens of "what I have to give up," you are each making decisions that support the deeper underlying needs of yourself and the person you love.

POWER PLAYS AT WORK

In your relationships at work, you'll use your personal power to establish boundaries, effectively communicate with others, and develop healthy interactions with coworkers, supervisors, direct reports, and clients. Your ability to manage these relationships is crucial to achieving your professional goals and making what you want happen.

Without a doubt, seeking connection through shared objectives and supporting one another until everyone can celebrate their collective victories is an awesome way to play. However (just as with a reluctant spouse at home), not everyone collaborates and cooperates commendably in the same sandbox. Power plays happen at work all the time. Knowing how power is being used by a colleague, customer, or your boss will grant you an enormous advantage when using your own personal power. It helps you formulate a more thoughtful or strategic response when someone pulls a power move on you.

Some people get assigned power instantly through their title. In a business setting, if you're a C-suite executive (CEO, CFO, COO, etc.) or a president or managing director, your title implies that you have legitimately been appointed power through your position. This title doesn't make you a leader, though. In fact, it doesn't guarantee you anything but a temporary title if you don't wield your power well. Earning followers' support or respect, or frankly just getting squat from them, requires special skills and talents: in your subject-matter expertise, in your self-awareness, and in your awareness of others. Strengthening your personal power means investing in your own credibility and knowledge set. It also includes bolstering your emotional intelligence skills and your communication skills so you can positively influence others and get things done. Additionally, it requires keeping your ego in check. You can't lead if no one will follow.

Leaders who are low in people and persuasion skills often use coercion or threats to get their way or increase their leverage. These bullies diminish trust inside an organization and drain the culture of good energy. Getting sucked into a power play and being a doormat are the two extremes to avoid.

The first way to respond to an overt power play is to remember that you are not defined by your title and neither are they. You are not defined by your paycheck and neither are they. You are not anybody's definition of you, except your own. This person, no matter what "authority" they think they may have, does not have authority over your identity and self-worth. Whenever someone tells me "But I have no choice. They're my boss," I remind them that they always have a choice. Each one of us is 100 percent responsible for our own life. Whenever a senior business executive dangerously thinks, *They have to do it. They work for me*, either their tenure will be short-lived, their employees will eventually leave, or everyone will plod along in lockstep with the company's slow growth. Inspiring and engaging commitment is not the same as demanding compliance.

The second-best way to respond to a power play at work

is to *flow with* instead of *fight against* someone's power play. The most effective techniques for *flowing with* are responses that reduce adversarial tension instead of escalating it.

- Thanks for the feedback. I'll take your recommendations under advisement.
- You've shared three different priorities, and I want to ensure I meet your expectations. Which one should I prioritize first?
- You sound frustrated. If I have contributed to your frustration, I apologize. That was not my intent. How might we best move forward?
- Let's work through this approach together so we can resolve it successfully.
- Let's define what a successful outcome looks like...
- Let's agree to next steps...
- Is this a definitive decision, or are we exploring options?

Taking the high road may not be easy, but when a person can no longer use their power to dominate you, they frequently stop. You've taken the "fun" out of their game.

You may need to respond to a power play by standing your ground. If the responses above do not decrease the tension and you're at risk of being a doormat or, worse, being abused, then it's time to directly address the inappropriate behaviors. When confronting a power monger, prepare ahead of time and conduct the conversation privately. Frame the conversation to gather more information and, ironically, to connect. Yes, your best initial power move is to start with connection, unless of course the power play is sexual or discriminatory. Then you'll get out a can of professional *whup-ass* and assert your power full force.

Keeping to less ghastly but still unacceptable behaviors, suppose you have a boss who is a bit of a tyrant. Beginning a conversation with the line "You can't yell at me anymore" often won't get you what you want long-term. Starting with, "I wanted to talk with you today because this project means a lot to me. I'm committed to making it happen. I've been surprised lately by the number of times we've interacted under stressful conditions. Yesterday, a part of me felt you were critical about our deadlines, and last week you were visibly upset about the budget. I sincerely want to better understand what you're thinking so we can reduce the tension between us" is a more constructive way to frame the conversation.

Affirming a boss or colleague's perspective and position can go a long way toward behavioral change. If the power player feels better understood personally or recognized for their positional power, it can help you *flow with* their wants. Adding any of the following lines to your tough conversation will allow you to more advantageously *flow to* your request at the same time.

- I imagine you're juggling a highly demanding client, and I realize that this is only one project on your plate. It must be stressful. How might I better help?
- How might I better assure you that my pieces of this project will be done and done right?
- I appreciate your willingness to sit down with me. I care very much about my contributions here, and I'm a better contributor when there's less tension. Today has helped me to understand where you're coming from. Thank you for listening to where I'm coming from.
- Going forward, I want to request that you and I communicate calmly and respectfully with one another.

Entering a tough conversation to stop a power play starts with connection. When you attempt to better understand the situation from your boss or colleague's perspective, it's easier for them to honor yours. When you *flow with* and take the high road, you can often get a solid outcome for both parties. However, if you seek to connect and set a boundary and it gets trespassed on, you will need to either be more direct in your request or offer, call in for reinforcement, or choose to take a different course of action. Being a pawn for someone else is most definitely not what you want. Your best power play when the gamer is out of control is to decline to play at all or change the game altogether. Unfortunately, some situations, sometimes, are beyond resolution. You may decide to abandon the situation completely or put up with it as best you can until you can create a better path forward. Some people are unmovable and unreasonable for a variety of reasons, but there are better ways to get what you want than to suffer abuse at the hands of others.

TECHNICAL FOUL–HARASSMENT AND OTHER SERIOUS TRANSGRESSIONS ON THE JOB

When someone complains to you about another organizational member who is using power-play behavior that is sexist, racist, sexually inappropriate, or discriminatory, you will of course want to respond by showing you take their concerns seriously. You will need to help them with the necessary steps to ensure their concern gets to the right people so the situation can be promptly investigated and thoroughly addressed. Serious note: whether or not you initially know the full story, you will legally need to report it, and you can still ask:

- How might I best support you?
- What are you hoping we might do together first?

Maybe they want your help in taking the issue to HR; maybe they want your ideas on how to approach the issue with the offender. Asking how you can support them allows you to get clear on what they're hoping will happen next. That doesn't mean that you have to agree to their request, but it may help you find the right person to assist them if that person isn't you.

If someone shares information with you that violates company policy but follows up their concern with, "I'm just sharing. I just wanted you to know. Please don't say anything," your best response is:

> I am so glad you shared, and I'm listening. You need to take this to HR immediately so they can do something about it. I will even go with you if you'd like. Based on what you've told me, I want this to be resolved, and I will need to share this with HR. How can we do that together in a comfortable way?

This person may understandably be scared or feel betrayed by your perceived unwillingness to hold their confidence. Furthermore, in some circumstances, if you are in a management position, you're actually required by law to share the information and take steps to address it.

If you are a boss or leader and are hearing for the first time about a transgression that you cannot confirm or deny, do not take sides in your initial response. This person might be offended that you're not going to bat for them by immediately aligning yourself with them and condemning their accused. A comment such as "Our company's core values do not condone statements (or actions) like those you've shared" is a good way to express that what you're hearing is far from acceptable nor will it ever be tolerated. However, you don't have enough information to comment beyond what little you know. Remember, what you want is a safe, respectful work environment for everyone. When you do share this information, it will be important that legal structures are in place to respect the rights of all involved and to support actions taken.

WEARING YOUR OWN CAPE

When someone's deplorable power play is toward you, you may struggle to use your personal power. Sometimes you're so shocked by someone's words or actions that your own voice is momentarily silenced or your body is momentarily paralyzed. Please give yourself grace. It's so easy to have twenty-twenty hindsight. *Why didn't I say this? Why didn't I do that? What was I thinking?* are naturally self-incriminating refrains and not beneficial. Beating yourself up makes you an innocent target...a second time. Once was enough.

What you may find more supportive and constructive is to remind yourself that you can choose to still address the incident or issue once you've gathered your wits about you and regained your composure. You may return to the offender with a comment along the lines of:

- Yesterday (or last Friday) I was so taken aback by your remark, I didn't know how best to respond. Today I want to address it directly.
- The other day, your behavior was so upsetting (disturbing, offensive, inappropriate, rude, hurtful), I didn't know how best to respond. Today I want to address it directly.

If quite a bit of time has passed since the event took place and you're still troubled or distracted by it, it's not too late. You have every right to get the peace you want and the closure you may need with comments such as:

I thought I could let this go and move forward; however, I'm not able to drop it. Clearly it matters to me. I need to share with you that what took place last spring (last fall, last year, two years ago) was so upsetting (disturbing, offensive, inappropriate, rude, hurtful), I didn't know how best to respond. Today I want to address it directly.

If speaking directly with the offender is too unsettling for you, ask for help. If you're feeling uncertain about your own ability to respond, or you're feeling like your own cape is a little rusty or dusty, call for backup. No one is coming to your aid unless you call for reinforcements.

Ask for help from someone who can assist you in preparing for a conversation where you address the offender and assert your own personal power, or ask for help from someone who can take action to ensure your safety and get you the appropriate support you need to stop egregious power plays. Asking for help is not weak; it's an awesome power play for giving you exactly what you want—knowing your own self-worth.

A MAGICAL PHRASE FOR STEP 2: *THAT MAKES SENSE TO ME*

So many strange altercations and romantic entanglements have been thwarted due to the charming spell of these words. Picture two lovers arguing. One is thinking *You're crazy* but instead says, "That makes sense to me," and suddenly seasons change, moods swing, and hot sex is back on the table. Yep, this phrase is a game changer, my pixie dusters.

First, not everything makes sense. Politics. Money. Why so many dog owners look like their pets. How that gal ended up with that guy—don't even get me started. Not to mention your Uncle Julio's conspiracy theories. Dangnabbit, and now he gets a little more credit for that alien thing, which has him more fired up than ever. As your aunt says, "He's crazier than a bedbug white-water rafting down your sheets." But the next time your uncle shares his inner thoughts out loud, if you want to see him look totally pleased and a bit perplexed, use this magical phrase on him. The moment he finishes telling you, "I was the original Adam. God sent me back again to save all apple trees from future harm and to save the human race," just nod and say, "That makes sense to me."

Second, not everything needs to make complete sense to you. The question for you is, can you see it making sense for them? From *their* perspective, are they making sense? If you set aside your judgments and condemnation and unroll your skeptical eyes, can you see it from their point of view? If you're feeling compassionate and genuinely care about this person and your connection with them, and you still do not *get* what they are trying to tell you, say, "Tell me more. I sincerely want to understand."

This response gives them an opportunity to more fully explain. The goal is to genuinely understand so you may extend empathy and connect. Everyone wants to have a witness, to be understood and heard. When someone shares their perspective, their truth, and you respond affirmingly with, "That makes sense to me," it does not mean you necessarily agree with them. It does not mean you must believe their truth too. It only means that what they are sharing *does* make sense to you. From their perspective, you can understand and appreciate why they perceive a situation or subject the way they do. You do not have to agree to validate their truth. This response simply indicates that you understand the logic of what the other person is saying from their point of view.

It's not lying to say to someone, "That makes sense to me," even when you disagree with them. Stepping into their shoes to fully appreciate and better understand their perspective doesn't mean you now have to believe something entirely different. It only means that their truth makes much more sense to you when you widen your lens. You weren't lying to your Uncle Julio either. He said he was back from biblical times to save apples and the human race. You said, "That makes sense to me." And it does make sense to you. Why? Because you know your Uncle Julio is a nut-jay. From his perspective and yours, it makes sense.

WE'RE ALL A SKOSH MISTAKEN

Humans are designed to believe there is just one "reality"—theirs. It is also one of life's greatest illusions. The truth is, you have your own unique reality. You have your own legitimate experience of the world in any given situation, and your "reality" is just as valid as another's, even though it might not be factually correct.

Most adults accept the idea that you and I each have our own equally valid reality. But in a committed relationship, once things slip into a cycle of sarcasm, frustration, aggression, anger, or withdrawal, you may become so focused on self-preservation that you lose your ability to see the validity of your partner's perspective, much less feel empathy for it.

With practice, this phrase will help you talk about the toughest topics with such a high degree of confidence that you and your partner will leave the conversation feeling more heard and understood than when it began. It is designed to break down emotional walls, reduce conflict, and restore connection and empathy.

When your partner is sharing his or her deepest misgivings or painful wounds and you say, "Pass the ketchup, get over it, let bygones be bygones" or, worse, "I don't understand you," your partner does not feel heard, accepted, or loved. On the other hand, when partners experience renewed mutual understanding, empathy, and connection, they feel safe. When partners feel safe, it is much easier for them to resolve conflict. One of the very best ways to make your partner feel safe is to say:

- That makes sense to me.
- You make sense because...
- That makes sense; I can see where...
- I can understand what you're saying because...

These magical phrases are designed to help you and your partner move out of reactivity and back to a place of mutual understanding, respect, acceptance, and love. Which is really what we all so very much want in our most intimate relationship.

ANOTHER MAGICAL PHRASE FOR STEP 2: *A PART OF ME...*

One of my most favorite one-liners to reduce tension in a tough conversation and lower the other person's defenses is: "A part of me..."

This phrase is a brilliant way to express a negative emotion you are feeling while simultaneously creating space for other emotions and possible solutions. Whether you're upset with a partner, frustrated with one of your kids, fed up with an underperformer at work, or dealing with a difficult sibling, it's important to *not* speak in absolutes.

When you say, "I'm frustrated" or "I'm disappointed," the other person hears an absolute. There's no wiggle room for other emotions. It's as if you just said, "I'm one hundred percent frustrated" or "I'm one hundred percent disappointed." Whereas, when you say,

- A part of me is frustrated...
- A part of me is disappointed...

you're communicating that it's not your only emotion. You're also leaving wiggle room for respect, hope, love, and connection.

The next time your teenager misses a curfew, instead of blowing your gasket, respond with:

- A part of me is angry that you're late...
- A part of me is disappointed in your choices...
- A part of me is very relieved that you are home safe, and a part of me is angry that you're late.
- A part of me is happy that you have friends to hang with, and a part of me is disappointed in your choice to ignore our agreement.

These phrases communicate to your teen that you are displeased but you haven't stopped loving her. A bonus consequence of any of these phrases is that they reduce the need for your teen to fight or flee. Absolutes tend to raise tension and incite defensiveness because the other person feels like they have no room to move. If you say to your teenage daughter, "I'm angry!" She perceives it as, *You're angry? Well, I'm angry, too, about this immature curfew, so let's get ready to rumble.* Or she may react with the thought, *You're angry? Great, there's nothing I can do but try to escape your wrath.* This thought is then followed by her stomping off and slamming her bedroom door or slinking off and hoping you forget about her existence.

None of these outcomes is desirable nor gets you what you really want, which is to have your daughter come home safe and on time.

When you express one emotion as a part of an overall mix, then there's room for other emotions too. When you use the phrase *A part of me...,* tension de-escalates because you've opened the door for other, more positive feelings, and you've created space for dialogue instead of defensiveness. If you're not ready to talk because you are too upset in the moment or too tired, you may also say:

> A part of me is too tired to have a conversation with you right now. Let's sit down tomorrow morning. I want to hear about what happened tonight with your friends that caused you to miss your curfew.

You then give yourself time to cool off, you plant the seed that she might want to think about her choices, and you buy yourself time to strategize on how best to get what you want.

DECISIONS, DECISIONS, DECISIONS: WHAT SHOULD YOU DO?

The phrase *A part of me...* is also helpful for decision-making. When you honor that there are multiple wants within a decision you need to make, it's easier to explore the underlying needs and make more well-informed, aligned decisions that deliver what you want.

Imagine you are offered a new job. A part of you wants to accept the new job offer because it means a promotion. A part of you does not. A part of you loves the idea of taking on exciting new projects, but another part of you is not thrilled with the longer commute and the idea of getting to know a bunch of new team members who will all have their own unique set of quirks. You decide to meet with your boss and see what new projects might be coming down the pike before you make the leap and accept the offer. There might be greener pastures right where you're standing.

Perhaps a part of you wants to go to the neighborhood barbecue this weekend, and a part of you wants to decline. A part of you knows Dan hosts a mean barbecue, but the neighborhood includes Bob. Bob's a blowhard and says such obnoxious things about everything and everyone, it's hard to eat Dan's burgers without getting indigestion. A part of you wants to go, but a part of you wonders if it's worth it. The more you think about the burgers, the more you salivate, but the more you think about Bob's inappropriate remarks, the more you lose your appetite. But dang it, Dan's a grill maestro! You decide to go. You practice saying a few one-liners to stop Bob in his tracks. On your walk over, crudité in hand, you remind yourself that Bob may be a buzzkill, but he will not kill your love of barbecue!

You're ready for a vacation. Understatement of the year. A part of you wants to go to the mountains for your next vacation, and a part of you wants to tour a city's multiple museums and restaurants. A part of you longs for the mountains because a big part of you is exhausted and burned out. A part of you wants to go to a cool city and do some urban exploring because a part of you is bored and in need of cultural stimulation. Taking the time to explore both parts of your vacation desires helps you plan a vacation in an awesome city not too far away from some adventures in nature. You're now more excited for this upcoming trip than ever before because you are getting everything you want, including reservations at the hip new bistro that is getting rave reviews online.

TUNING IN TO THE ROUGH AND TOUGH EMOTIONS

A part of me... also honors the myriad of emotions you are experiencing in response to certain tough life situations. Using this phrase helps you process your grief, stress, and anxiety; regain your equilibrium; and strengthen your resiliency. Life is messy. It can be tragic. It can be downright cruel. In response to a death, divorce, betrayal, or a significant change in your life, you will experience more than one emotion. *I'm sad* is not as comprehensive of all you're going through as *A part of me is grieving and I feel such loss, and at the same time a part of me is relieved. She was in so much pain.*

I'm angry! is not as all-embracing as saying, *A part of me is furious and insulted, and a part of me is stunned and hurt.*

When you get clear on all of the emotions you are experiencing, it is easier to process through them individually. Sorting through each separate sentiment gives you the gift of gaining greater clarity on what it is you now truly need and want. Over time, your responses and wants will shift. Staying tuned in to your responses will help you heal, process, and move forward as a stronger person. Consistently checking in with yourself at each phase and stage of a tough experience will help you ask for and get what you need and want.

DERAILED BUT NOT DONE

Anna's marriage was sliding down the slippery slope of dissatisfaction, and it was more than just a slump. Unless slumps could last for a couple years. Then, yes, they were definitely in a slump. A sexless slump. A no-fun slump. A nagging slump. It'd been ages since they'd had fun, and she couldn't recall the last time she and her hubby had stayed up connecting with awesome pillow talk. They needed to get their relationship back on track. Anna's list of wants was lengthy. She wanted more fun, more sex, and more intimacy. She also wanted to feel like her bestie had her back and that he actually gave a rip. She wanted to feel wanted. She wanted this relationship to work. She wanted it to last. She loved her husband. He was her lover (technically, nonlover at the moment, but she didn't want to be rude about it), and she wanted their connection back.

When Anna looked at the relationship from Greg's perspective, she was more uncertain about what he might be thinking these days than she'd originally thought. She was fairly sure sex and fun would be on his list, too, but as "no" was the answer she got from him the last two times she hinted at ignoring the television and moving to the bedroom, she wasn't too sure what was going through his mind lately. She hoped Greg still loved her. She hoped he felt loved by her. Hmmm. Anna bit her lip. She wondered if her bestie *really* did feel loved by her right now. D'oh! She closed her eyes. Not if she were to go by their latest argument about the recycling bin and last week's snarky exchange about the electric bill. Yeah, she sorta overreacted on that one.

Anna knew it was time to have a heart-to-heart conversation, but starting with "Honey, we need to talk," would pretty much ensure their conversation was dead on arrival. She didn't want Greg to feel like he was being called to the principal's office. He wasn't in trouble, but he wasn't exactly going to be given a green participation ribbon either. Framing where she wanted to end up long-term seemed daunting to her as well. "Greg, we must get happy and stay together forever. I will not let you leave me." Uh, definitely no. She didn't want to frighten him away.

Anna recalled the old adage: a guy wants sex to feel connected and a gal wants to feel connected in order to have sex. It seemed like a no-win catch-22 to her, until she reminded herself it wasn't the only option on the table. They needed to start with having fun. Maybe they could go see a comedian's stand-up show together and literally laugh out loud. Maybe she could buy tickets to a baseball game and they could splurge on overpriced hotdogs, or they could volunteer at their favorite charity and then hit the beach and kayak with friends. She wanted to pick an activity that reminded them both they knew how to smile in one another's company. Anna knew that turning things around would happen one conversation at a time, and hashing things out would be better after they'd reconnected.

Anna mapped out possible opening frameworks.

- How might we have fun this weekend? I'm thinking a baseball game or kayaking. What are you thinking?

🌸 Hey, Boo, let's have fun this weekend. What sounds the most fun to you?

If he wasn't at all on board with having fun, then she would pull out a life preserver, starting with:

Hey, Boo, a part of me is nervous that maybe we're drifting too far apart. I love you. Would you be willing to sit down with our favorite takeout and open up a bottle of wine so we can reconnect tonight and talk about having more fun and getting anchored again?

The flow of their conversation would be honest but not brutal, and it would begin to move them toward her stated outcome. Anna would focus on her desire to reconnect, have more fun, and put hot sex back on the agenda. The kind of sex where they both actually removed their oversized T-shirts and she stopped thinking about the calories she was burning instead of the pleasure they were experiencing. This first conversation was not the time to complain; it was the time to reconnect.

To increase her connection with Greg, Anna was going to need to decrease her belief that her story was the only story. She was raised by parents who would be celebrating their thirty-seven-year anniversary next month. They never fought. Okay, more honestly, she admitted, they didn't fight in front of her. She'd only ever seen them be respectful toward each other, and they still held hands when they took a walk. This is how she wanted her marriage with Greg to be. From her perspective, Greg's parents were more...uninspiring. They seemed to go through the motions of marriage without too much incident, but she'd always disliked their apathy toward one another. Their marriage model was not one Anna wanted to emulate for herself and Greg. She wondered, however, if Greg might instinctively be operating from his comfort zone of "This is the only version of marriage I know," and she was operating from an entirely different comfort zone of "This is the only version I know." Until she asked him to share his stories and expectations about marriage, she could only guess.

Anna sighed. It was so tempting to just yell at him, "This stinks. Why can't you get off the couch and act interested in me?" But she knew better. She wanted Greg to feel secure and loved, not criticized or attacked. She brainstormed possible scripts that focused on connection.

- Boo, last year when we went to all those baseball games, we had such a good time. Thank you for making that happen. We haven't done anything like that in a while. I want to put some fun energy back into our lives. What would be most fun for you in the next few months?
- Boo, I love you so much. A part of me is scared that

maybe we're getting into a rut that's not healthy. A part of me is worried that it's been a while since I've seen that look that means you want to jump my bones. I'm not sure how to get it back. Does this make sense to you?

She decided if things were so bad that heading out for an activity they both normally enjoyed sounded like purgatory to Greg, then it would be time to dive into a more intimate conversation. Suggesting couples' therapy might be a needed and appropriate request at some point, but Anna knew it wasn't an ideal way to start. She chuckled just imagining kicking off a conversation with, "Boo, we're a mess. Our relationship has crashed on the rocks of reality and the only thing that can save us is a couple's retreat filled with lots of affirmations, incense, and eye contact." *No way,* she thought, making herself grin. Greg would run for the hills. Seeking professional counseling might indeed be in their cards, and she knew both of them would agree to go if asked, but first she owed it to herself, to him, and to their marriage to stop avoiding this needed conversation.

Throughout their talk, she could ask questions that generated positivity, intimacy, and shared understanding. She brainstormed a long list of possible questions and then selected several to rekindle their connection.

- What do you and I each cherish most about our relationship?
- From your perspective, what was one of the best days we had together in the last six months?
- What contributed to this day being your choice?
- What was one of the most fun activities we did together in the last year?
- How do we each define an ideal marriage?
- Where are we aligned in our definitions?
- How might we honor our differences?
- How might we reconnect and create more "ideal" time together?
- What's the benefit/payoff when we have fun together?
- What's the benefit/payoff when we have more connectivity?
- How might we begin to get more play in our relationship?
- How might we prioritize dates?
- How might we spark more romance and sex?
- How might we best move forward? What's the first and best next step?

Anna felt much better about approaching their relationship drift by focusing on connection first. If she began with their strengths as a couple, she could help both of them acknowledge that all was not lost and good things were happening. Things might be off, but the relationship was not caught in a total quagmire of failure and dysfunction. From a place of pluses, she would focus on her commitment to him and their relationship as a whole. They could then move into alignment and future tweaks to get more of what they each wanted. Anna felt her shoulders relax. It was the first time in a long while she felt hope for their future.

GET WHAT YOU WANT: CONNECTION OR POWER

First, are you choosing connection or power? On a rare occasion, it may be both. If you need to lean in, your words and actions will be different than if you need to strengthen your spine.

AM I SEEKING CONNECTION OR POWER?

I need to lean in and connect with ....

or

I need to assert my personal power with ....

Second, the emotions and energy you physically choose to display and verbally voice will affect your interactions not only with others but also with yourself. You will either feel heard, understood, and accepted or you won't. They will either feel heard, understood, and accepted or they won't. There's not much wiggle room. You will either aim to create connection or assert your personal power. Another person's response is not completely within your control, but it is within your sphere of influence. Get clear on how you wish to present yourself and the emotions and energy you wish to display.

Listing out all your emotions and deciding which ones are the most important for you to convey is a great therapeutic exercise for you and prevents you from serving up an emotional tsunami during the conversation. Your list of emotions may be quite long, but expressing your top three to four most prioritized sentiments will suffice. Sharing feelings such as you're *still in love*, and you're also *scared* and *uncertain about the future*, conveys a great deal of information without overwhelming the other person.

I'M FEELING...

....

....

....

....

....

Which emotions are most important to me to convey?

Third, people hear what you want them to know and feel from *what* you say and *how* you say it. Choosing how you show up and present yourself is as important as the words you use. A condescending and judgmental tone or a reasonable request expressed through a petulant, stubborn pitch can ruin the most artfully crafted prose. Just as a snarky zinger can undo all the goodwill that was created, so can a fitting demeanor rectify a tenuous situation.

When you're close to someone, you might be tempted to jump into the conversation with your unmet wants. "I'm so upset. We never go out anymore. We never make love." There indeed might be some truth to what you're sharing, but *how* you share your truth is critical for establishing empathy and connection. While it may be appealing to start with everything that's broken and not working, or that you find offensive about the other party, showing up with an optimistic attitude and a willingness to own your piece will move you toward a heartfelt resolution more quickly.

- What energy do I need to bring to this conversation?
- What feelings do I wish to communicate through words and physical presence? (A part of me feels...)
- What emotions am I attempting to incite in them? (calm, acceptance, certainty, safety, love, urgency, respect, etc.)

- What might I say or do to foster empathy?
- What might I say or do to create connection?
- What might I say or do to assert my personal power?

Additionally, the stakes are too high in your personal relationships, especially your most intimate one, to be playing guessing games. The more you explore another's stories, the more their words and actions will make sense to you. Your significant other has a belief system that may or may not be aligned with yours. If not aligned, you won't be able to merge your disparate belief systems through logic. You'll only be able to merge them when the two of you co-create a new belief system that works for the both of you.

- How does what's currently happening make sense from their perspective? (You don't have to agree with them or condone their words and actions to better understand what's motivating their choices.)
- What questions might I ask them to better understand their thoughts, stories, and beliefs?

Find your words. Be you. These questions are designed to guide your own style. Be sure to remove all judgments, accusations, and absolutes. Stay positive and forward-focused and aim to set the right tone and tenor. Lastly, if you are awkward, if you stumble a bit, if you're surprised by the emotions that suddenly show up, just say, "Clearly this matters to me."

There's no need to apologize for reddened cheeks, teary eyes, a tight throat, or any other physical responses. They are symptoms of one simple fact: you care about this relationship.

Last but not least, it's important to be direct and clear with your asks. Hoping that your partner will miraculously intuit what you're thinking and feeling is not going to get you what you want. Over the years, I've heard grown people utter ridiculously un-grownup phrases, such as "We've been together for twenty years. She should know what I need." "If he really knew me, he'd know what to do," and one of my all-time favorites, "He should just know. If I ask, then it's like he's just giving me what I asked for." Um, that's the point. Asking for what you need is your responsibility, which means you need to verbalize it clearly.

- I'm asking for...
- I need...
- I really want...

Seeking connection includes inquiring about their needs.

- If you could ask for anything, what would it be?
- What do you need most from me or from us right now?
- What do you really want?

The best questions and key phrases you choose will align with your desired outcome and your intent to reunite. Demonstrating your willingness to change your own behaviors or take action to get what you want goes a long way toward influencing your partner's willingness to do the same. The magic of your wand in Step 2 expands in direct proportion to how much you prepare and practice asking for what you really want, whether it be through seeking greater connection or asserting your personal power.

TUNE IN TO ALL THE CONVERSATIONS

Sean was incensed. The more he listened to his daughter Leila describe her basketball game over the phone, the more infuriated he got. She loved the sport. As a family, they'd played it together for years in the driveway, but her passion was waning. All because of her high school coach. He played favorites, and he was a screamer. His face would turn bright red, his fists would flail, and he'd been kicked out of quite a few games over the years. Last summer, Sean and his wife, Mia, looked at other high schools where their daughter might play, but the politics of switching schools as a rising junior in a fairly small town was a beast they didn't wish to tackle. "Dad" was regretting this decision, though. He listened to Leila share how Coach, once again, played favorites with his own daughter, Tammy, in tonight's game. Tammy was a junior as well, but team captain, mildly talented, and enthusiastically lazy, and she started tonight in spite of missing practice twice in the last week. Sean's daughter was furious because she knew if she'd even been so much as a minute late to a practice, her butt would have been on the bench the whole first half of the game.

What sent Sean over the edge was when Leila mentioned that Coach publicly shamed her after their game. Apparently, Coach had declared in front of the whole team that it was Leila's turnover in the fourth quarter that almost cost them the game. This was after she'd scored eighteen points, two of which were three-pointers. Sean raked his hands through his hair. Just hours earlier, he had been upset with himself for traveling and missing her game, but now he wondered if it was a blessing in disguise. If he'd been there, he might have said something he'd regret.

"Leila, slow down. Repeat that," Sean said, realizing he was so caught up in his own thoughts he hadn't heard her last few sentences.

"I want to go to the athletic director, Dad. I want to tell Mr. Martin what Coach is doing. It's bad enough that he cost us last week's games with two technicals before they kicked him out, but tonight was blatant nepotism. We were down fourteen at the half. Not only did Tammy start after missing two practices, he only took her out of the game once. She's the one that almost cost us the game, not me."

Sean took a breath. Yet her team had won. According to his daughter, she and her best friend, Nyah, had dominated in the second half, scoring twenty-seven points between them to turn it around. As much as he agreed with Leila, it was more complicated than a single conversation with Eric Martin, the athletic director. First, Martin had hired Coach. Second, Coach had played Martin's daughter for three years, despite her lack of skill. Third, a couple of the parents whose girls played a lot were happy to overlook his transgressions. Despite all of his spectacularly unacceptable behaviors, and the fact that most families despised his yelling and theatrical tantrums, he was known as a winning coach. This was what made it so hard. Coach had won league champion more years than he had not. A letter of recommendation from him and his support in helping Leila get a scholarship were needed. Sean sighed. There were so many layers to unpack. Too many possible consequences and potentially unintended consequences were at stake.

"Dad? Are you going to go with me? I hate playing for him. I busted my butt all week, and Tammy started. We almost lost. If Nyah and I hadn't swept up, we'd have been dirt all over that floor. Mr. Martin needs to know, Dad. Dad?"

"Baby," he said slowly, "we need to look at all the conversations that are gonna be going down before we just go waltzing into Martin's office." Sean leaned back on the hotel bed and rubbed his eyes. Somehow the high-stakes deal he was finalizing tomorrow seemed like child's play compared to his child's actual play. As Mia had said, "We signed up for basketball, but most weeks, we're playing chess."

THE EGO HOOK

There's never just one conversation happening. Whether you're conversing with a boss, a neighbor, your spouse, or your kid's coach, there are multiple conversations taking place simultaneously. If you're not aware of all these conversations, things can get messy, or worse, one of these conversations might bite you in the butt. When preparing for a tough conversation, it's critical to remember that there's the conversation between the two of you, the conversation going on inside *your* head, and the conversation going on inside *their* head. Add another person to the party, and you've just added their internal conversation and even more wants to the mix.

Everyone has a ticker tape of thoughts inside their head. While you are physically engaged in a conversation with someone, their internal conversation is flying by at the bottom of their brain screen. Sometimes these thoughts are aligned with yours and focused on the topic at hand. This alignment is very helpful in getting you what you want. Alas, other times, their thoughts are far away from the topic at hand, or worse, they're in direct opposition to the conversation taking place.

The most common detrimental conversation that's taking place at the exact time you are dialoguing with someone is called the Ego Hook. There are two versions of the Ego Hook conversation: the other person's and yours. The other person's Ego Hook conversation starts the second they ask themselves, *What does this conversation say about me?*

Imagine a manager named Bill is frustrated with his colleague Tom. Bill's had it. No matter how many times he meets with Tom, Tom just isn't getting it. Bill meets with his boss, Doug, and says, "Tom is an idiot. I can't work with him. What are we gonna do? It's as if Tom thinks he can swim without getting wet. It's driving me nuts."

On the surface, it appears that Bill is having a conversation with his boss, Doug, about Tom. That's only one of the conversations in play. There's also the conversation Doug is having with himself. One of the hardest components of a tough conversation is preparing for the secondary conversation going on inside the other person's head: *What does this conversation say about me?*

Imagine Doug thinking to himself as Bill stands in front of him and calls Tom an idiot: *You think Tom is an idiot. I hired Tom. Maybe you're suggesting I'm an idiot too. Maybe this is your way of saying you think I'm not a good manager. Tom's not easy, but calling him an idiot...that's rough. And I'm sure as heck not an idiot!*

Instead of staying open-minded, actively listening, and engaging in constructive problem-solving with Bill, Doug's defenses go up. His ego is threatened. When an ego is threatened or hooked, it wants to know the answers to three very specific questions:

1. Am I competent?
2. Am I a good person?
3. Am I still respected, accepted, or loved?

Our egos operate from a very matter-of-fact, either-or perspective of absolutes, such as *I'm creative. I'm responsible. I'm smart. I'm mature.* When someone tells us we did or said something that was lame, irresponsible, dumb, or immature, our egos implode and we think, *No way, that's not me!* An ego has the potential to live much of its existence in a state of denial.

It's important to consider what ego issues you might be triggering in the person you're talking to if you're going to lead a conversation to the profitable outcome you're trying to obtain. Might the person you're talking to get their ego hooked and hear you calling them a bad boss, an insensitive spouse, a lousy parent, a rotten coach, or an inept lover? Ouch! Planning how you might frame the conversation to reduce the likelihood of you triggering someone's ego is a brilliant way to increase the likelihood of getting what you want.

In the case of Bill and Doug, Bill would be wise to reassure his boss with a conversation starter such as "I know Tom's got some tremendous strengths. I understand and appreciate the significance of his role. My goal in this conversation is to share my thoughts around a specific issue, hear your thoughts around this issue, and then strategize together how we might get through this without creating more damage." Bill might then share two or three specific examples of how Tom's behaviors created collateral damage. With that opener, Doug is much more likely to listen and actively engage than get caught up in his own internal ego-hooked story.

YOUR EGO HOOK–GIVER

When it comes to your internal Ego Hook, there are two versions: giver and receiver. If you're the giver of bad news and what you need to share goes against your identity of who you think you are, your ego leans toward self-destructive behaviors. Giving a performance review and ending a relationship are two classic examples. If you feel like you're going to hurt someone's feelings and you typically perceive yourself as the nice guy or the nice gal, or the kindhearted manager, your ego may cave and undermine your original intentions. In the case of the performance review, you may soften the feedback or downplay it. You may be all set to share how your expectations are not being met, but the moment your employee tears up or turns red, you find yourself softening the feedback. Surprising your own ears, you hear yourself saying, "It's not that bad, George. Really, I'll see what I can do." You darn well know there's nothing you can do! You unfortunately just got Ego-Hooked.

Regarding your personal relationship, even though you know in your heart of hearts it's not the relationship for you, you may lose your courage to end it. You don't express your feelings, and you wind up staying way too long. Staying with someone too long because you don't want to hurt their feelings at first seems noble, but it's not. It's selfish and immature. It's actually about protecting your ego instead of altruistically caring enough about the other person to hurt them less today than next year. *I'm too nice, I'm too kind. How will he survive without me? I don't wanna be the bad one. I haven't met anyone else. I don't want to crush his spirit.* Sadly, these are all sentiments of your hooked ego, and they prevent you and the other person from getting the ideal relationship you both want.

Your ego can get hooked whenever you need to share upsetting news. The best rule to follow is to be honest. *Honesty is the best policy* is an adage for a reason. You don't need to be callous or rude, just thoughtful. Telling someone that sharing this news is harder for you than it will be for them is insincere. Telling someone whom you're firing that their dismissal will be a golden opportunity for them is not an appropriate epiphany for you to bequeath while simultaneously handing them a pink slip. On an airplane flight last year, a young boy in the row behind me was crying about losing a game to his older brother. I overhead his mom say, "You didn't want to win anyway." Hmmm. Pretty sure at the time both boys thought it was all about winning. It's more than appropriate to teach our kids that winning isn't everything, but it's disingenuous when you dismiss a real want. Before you offer up a trite platitude, ask yourself, *Who am I comforting, and are these words really going to help more than they hurt?*

YOUR EGO HOOK–RECEIVER

Ego Hooks can also happen to you when you're the recipient of bad news. If the feedback you get violates your ego, it will get instantly hooked. When you're triggered, it's important to remind yourself that this one instance doesn't define who you are. You can be responsible and do something irresponsible. You can be smart and do or say something really dumb. You can be creative and have a lame-idea day. One of the things to ask yourself when you find yourself on the defensive is, *In this instance, is there truth to what this person is saying? How might I have contributed to this outcome?* Friendly reminder—you're human. One misstep or transgression doesn't define the sum total of you.

If someone is giving you feedback that stings a little or if you feel defensive, recognize it as a self-protective move. Mentally say to yourself, *Okay, ego, the goal is to play better.* Then, if the person hooking your ego is someone you respect and trust, remind yourself that they have your back and want you to be successful. Even if *their* delivery wasn't the best, they want you to be *your* best. They're attempting to help. Feedback from a trusted source is useful. Whether the criticism is about the quality of your work, your results (or lack thereof), or your actions or inactions, their remarks provide a unique opportunity to learn about yourself or to learn about how others are perceiving you. For your ego's sake, reframe their criticism as insight and then discern how to best act on it.

On the flip side, if you don't know this person very well or don't respect this person, file their remarks in your brain's "just information" folder and decide later if their peanut gallery commentary is even relevant to you. Whether you use their "gift" of feedback or not is up to you, but you weren't raised by wolves, so simply say thank you. Now onward and upward.

Every now and then your ego may get triggered about a topic that you were already ruminating about. You're extra sensitive, which means you're more likely to be extra defensive. In this scenario you might reply to their feedback with, "I thought you might bring that up, and I'm thinking about that too. I'm wondering what I could have done differently or what I could have said that would have been better or made things easier." If your misstep caused an unintended consequence, step up and own it. Say "I've been thinking about that too, and I wish I had done...I sincerely apologize. This is a serious learning opportunity for me."

If someone turns the conversation spotlight back on your transgressions, you have the right to redirect the conversation back to the point at hand. Let's assume from the scenario above that Doug gets defensive and says, "Well, if you'd been a better mentor to Tom, this would never have happened." Instead of getting defensive, Bill ignores the bait. He responds with, "This conversation is not about me. I want to focus on Tom's behavior. I'm willing to explore my contributions next because I've been thinking about that, too, but first I want to stay focused on Tom's unwillingness to do these tasks and the unintended consequences it created." Bill's response is not defensive nor deflective. He stays the course and is much more likely to get what he wants than if he accepts Doug's invitation to slide down the blame-game rabbit hole.

BEING IN THE ZONE

With respect to Leila's precarious scenario, there were multiple egos that could have potentially gotten hooked. Sean wanted to support his daughter in using her voice, but he knew that *how* she used it would be imperative for a profitable outcome. He believed her desire to speak with the athletic director and coach was indeed a conversation worth having, he just wanted to help set her up for success. Yes, she absolutely needed to assert her personal power and address her concerns, but it was also important to do her best and not risk sacrificing her playing time or Coach's help in getting her a college scholarship. Obviously, Sean would support her speaking up no matter the outcome, but he was hoping to help her learn how to speak up without it costing her everything. Sean knew he needed to start by preparing for possible Ego Hooks, both with the athletic director and her coach. He also knew he needed to prepare his daughter for the various reactions she might trigger. He wished that the world was filled with more mature adults, but he knew wishful thinking wasn't going to get him or Leila what they wanted. They needed to turn this tough conversation into a highly profitable one, starting with getting all of them aligned.

Sean's brainstormed agenda:

- How might we define a "winning basketball team" both on and off the court? As an athletic director? A coach? A player? A parent?
- What are the current strengths of the girls' varsity basketball program?
- What's currently working?
- In addition to winning, what are the objectives of the program?
- What are some of our concerns about meeting and exceeding these objectives? As an athletic director? A coach? A player? A parent?
- How might we better close the gap between where we are today and where we want to be?

As Sean noodled through his questions, he noted where Martin and Coach might get defensive. He thought about his word choice carefully, aiming to connect with each man over their shared love of basketball and, more importantly, over their love for their respective daughters. This wasn't the conversation in which to list all of his grievances. Coach's behavior was immature and often offensive, but Sean wanted to first help Leila address her public belittling in the last game and her commitment to the team by showing up to practice—a commitment that he and Leila felt should be demonstrated by all. As he outlined his ideas, Sean made side notes about how to help his daughter find the right words and framing to get what she wanted. They were going to have a "pre-game" wand practice of their very own. Leila was going to practice her conversation skills as hard as she practiced basketball. She needed to know the Ego Hooks of every participant in the conversation, just as she knew the strengths and weaknesses of every player on her own team and the opposing teams.

WHERE YOU MIGHT GET STUCK

Picture everyone as the hero of his or her own movie. Depending on how their day is going, they might be starring in a rom-com, an action adventure, a mystery, a slow slice-of-life reel, a reality show, or dealing with a horror show. When you start a conversation with them, you are interrupting *their* movie. Everyone is starring in their own movie; even your dog has his own movie playing in his head.

Suppose your partner is in the middle of dealing with a difficult client. You interrupt her horror movie to drag her into your rom-com's third act "all is lost" scene. You're thinking your relationship is doomed unless she declares her undying love for you by stepping away from her laptop and prioritizing your wants. Her head spins and she responds with, "I may be working from home today, but can't you see I'm fighting off this crazy client who wants to hack me into pieces with his chainsaw-type negotiations?" Um, nope, you didn't see it. You're too absorbed in your own movie's scene, which is filled with a growling stomach, demanding children, finished conference calls, and an empty refrigerator.

Most of us start conversations from scenes in our movie with little regard for other people's movies. We bust into a conversation with, "I want to talk to you about..." and pitch our own needs and desires without consideration for others' needs. Oftentimes, when we start a conversation with our own requests, we *decrease* the likelihood of a profitable outcome, that is, getting exactly what we want.

When you're catching the other person in the middle of their own movie with a scene from yours, the best way to capture their interest is by making your conversation about *them* at first or finding a better time for intermission. Before you interrupt their regularly scheduled programming, ask yourself, *What's their desire? What's important to them? What might they want? Then how might I get us what we both want?* Once you've done your homework, you may then begin the conversation with their desired outcome as the opener to this new scene.

For example, perhaps you've invested a lot of time and energy on a professional project for the last three weeks. Your colleague is going to meet with the client tomorrow to bring her up to speed on your team's progress, and you want to ensure that your portion of the project is well represented. Most people would barge into their colleague's office and start the conversation with, "I want to talk to you about my piece of the project." Not you. You now have a communication wand, and you know how to wield it. Instead of starting with your own want, you send a quick email or text that begins with, "Hey, Stacy, since you're meeting with the client tomorrow, I thought I'd give you a brief update on where we're at with Phase Two. This way, you can be fully prepared to answer any of her questions and you can highlight what matters most to her. Let me know when it's a good time for us to touch base this afternoon, and I'll make it happen."

Now you've got your colleague's attention! Instead of an unwanted interruption, you're a lifesaver! Starting with the other person's desires will more often than not help you get whatever you desire.

A MAGICAL PHRASE FOR STEP 3: *I HAVE THIS STORY IN MY HEAD...*

Many stories are works of fiction. If you have family, you can relate. Everyone gathers together for the holidays or reunites for a significant generational milestone such as a wedding or graduation. Not long after the alcohol begins flowing, the reminiscing commences. Eventually, someone's version of how things "went down" years prior drastically differs from someone else's version. No one can believe the other person's story because they're so certain their version is correct. It makes for fun fodder and back-slapping hilarity unless it's a story about your pain and hurt. While everyone else finds the story uproariously comical, you burn with embarrassment as the butt of the joke.

Ironically, the only truth consistent in each person's version is how everyone has their own unique spin on it. You make up stories inside your head about the conflict you have with another, the trespasses that have been done against you, or the trespasses you've done unto others. You have a story about how ugly or beautiful people can be toward one another, how compassionate or cold they are to you, and how connected or isolated you feel.

When you get triggered by a life event, by some circumstance—whether it's a computer system crashing, a crash diet failing, or a presentation crashing and burning—you make up a story about it in your head. You develop a thought, and this thought causes you to feel a certain way. With these feelings, you take action, and these actions produce a result that proves your thought to be true. Your brain, the keeper of your thoughts, is a highly protective mechanism. It seeks out information to confirm, validate, and support the stories it creates. But what happens when your thoughts and stories aren't true? When the stories you have in your head make sense to you but may not be factually accurate? Without touching base with another or fact-checking yourself, you may move further and further away from what you want. Without realizing it, your unchecked story may move you in the opposite direction of where you wish to go.

MANY STORIES ARE MADE-UP MALARKEY

When I lived overseas, a friend of mine named Susie found herself smack-dab in the middle of a major mess. Susie was asked by one of her closest girlfriends, Jill, to do a favor for her. Jill wanted Susie to take her new boyfriend shopping for her Christmas present. Jill wanted Susie to help him pick out a gift that she'd be sure to like. Susie said yes. In early December, Susie spent an entire Saturday afternoon with Jill's new beau and helped him select three gifts she knew her friend would love. It took a lot longer than Susie expected, and, because of traffic, she was late to an event of her own that same evening.

The following Monday at work, Jill asked Susie how the shopping expedition went. Susie shared that they had a great time picking out gifts for her, but it had taken much longer than she anticipated. Susie emphasized again that it was fun, but also how much time it had taken out of her weekend. She was hoping Jill would realize that it was a bigger effort than they both had expected and thank her. Jill did not thank her. In fact, what Susie didn't realize until much later was that Jill started to wonder just how much fun Susie and her new boyfriend had on Saturday, especially as they sat in traffic together. Jill started developing this story in her head that maybe Susie liked her boyfriend.

Upon not getting a heartfelt thank you or seeing or hearing any signs of appreciation, Susie started to feel resentful toward Jill. She started a story in her head that Jill was selfish. Two days later, they ran into one another grabbing coffee in the cafeteria and Jill asked, "How many places did you two go before finding the gift?"

Susie replied, "A lot. We went everywhere. Actually, you have more than one gift from our day together. We spent hours at one store alone." Susie immediately felt silly. She quickly added, "But I was happy to do it. Really. We had fun." Susie's added lines were due to the other story in her head: *This friendship means a lot to me. I want to be thanked and appreciated, but I don't want to appear rude. I really did want to help you.*

Jill, with her own story of mistrust, only heard again how much fun they had together, and it reinforced her suspicions. This pattern went back and forth for two weeks until, one Sunday night, Jill called Susie crying. She shared that she and her boyfriend had an awful fight. Susie comforted her friend and said, "Oh, no, sweetie. I'm so sorry. Are you okay? Did you guys break up?" Susie's question triggered Jill's unchecked story. Jill angrily spat back, "No, we didn't break up; we had a fight. You'd love it if we had broken up, though, wouldn't you?!"

Susie was shocked. Then upset. Her story had a plot twist. Not only was her friend selfish, she was crazy. What did she mean, she'd be happy if they broke up? Had she not just spent an entire Saturday helping these two nincompoops have an awesome Christmas together? What a waste of her time and energy!

If Jill had shared with Susie, "I have this story in my head that maybe you like him..." then Susie could have explained, no, she didn't like him. She kept bringing it up because she wanted Jill to appreciate her time and effort in helping her.

If Susie had shared with Jill, "I have this story in my head that you don't care that it took as long as it did. That you don't appreciate what I did..." then Jill would have explained she was appreciative at first, but now she's wondering if it backfired. She's wondering how much fun they had together. Neither of these conversations would have felt like a summer breeze, but they certainly would have cleared the air and helped both of these women get what they wanted: a supportive, trusting friendship without the unnecessary drama of a bad movie.

When you share a story in your head, you frequently approach these conversations bombastically, aggressively, passive-aggressively, or defensively. You say things such as:

- You don't want to hang out with us anymore.
- You don't want me to be successful.
- Everything you do is about winning.
- You're jealous of my promotion.
- You're always undermining me.
- You're still upset about the other night.
- Nothing I ever say is good enough.
- You're trying to steal my boyfriend.

When you state your story as if it is fact, as if it is the only reality that could possibly exist, you risk fanning the flames of a fight. Rather than feeling more connected, accepted, and loved (which is what you really want when you share your story), you increase another's defensiveness and walls start going up—fast. Conversely, when you state your story as if it's a work in progress and open to modification, you make space for greater understanding. You're inviting further interpretations and a more complete perspective. When you say,

- I have this story in my head...
- I have this story in my head...I don't even know if it's true. I'm sharing it with you because I'm wondering if it's even accurate...

you aren't insisting you are right. In fact, you might very well just be imagining everything. This creates space for the possibility that you don't have it all figured out, and it gives the other party a chance to confirm or correct.

- I have this story in my head that you don't want to hang out with us anymore.
- I have this story in my head that you don't want me to be successful.
- I have this story in my head that winning might be the most important thing to you right now.
- I have this story in my head that you're jealous of my promotion.
- I have this story in my head that you're undermining me.
- I have this story in my head that you're still upset about the other night.
- I have this story in my head that what I say often isn't good enough.
- I have this story in my head that you're into my boy-friend.

You can then add:

◉ I wanted to check in with you and see if my story rings true.

Suppose you witness a series of behaviors exhibited by your spouse that you believe to be caused by a disagreement you had last week. You think you're interpreting these behaviors correctly, but maybe you're not. To you, your spouse is acting aloof, a bit removed, and distant. You've got this story in your head about what caused it. The next time your spouse appears distant you exclaim, "See! You're acting distant again. You've been ignoring me ever since the other night, and you simply won't admit it." Your spouse looks up, blinking at you from your blindsiding accusations and thinks, *What the—?*

Instead of ambushing someone with absolutes, share your story and check in to see if your story is even accurate.

◉ I have this story in my head that you're keeping your distance because you're still upset about the other night. Is there any truth to what I'm thinking?

When you say, "I have this story in my head..." you're offering an invitation to modify the story. If it's not a comforting story and there *is* truth to it, then it offers an invitation to resolve the tension, work through the problem, and change the final story.

CLIQUES ARE PAINFULLY CLICHÉ AT ANY AGE

I was coaching a young college student when she mentioned she was upset about some drama in her dorm. Several different cliques of girls had formed over the course of the semester and now one of her friends, who had joined another clique, was dismissing her a lot. As they had been great friends all year long, they had planned on spending a week of vacation time together over the summer. On the coaching call, my client expressed that she was seriously worried they would be miserable hanging out together. She asked me for advice on whether she should cancel her holiday plans and concluded with, "I want friends I can trust. I want to have fun with friends who are really my friends."

"You don't even know if your story is true," I responded. "It's super hard to make the right decision if you're not even sure you have the right story." I taught her this magical phrase, and she practiced role-playing.

"I have this story in my head that you don't want to hang out with me as much anymore. The last few weekends in a row, you've said no to every invitation. Now I'm wondering if you still want to hang out this summer. Am I reading you right or not?"

She took a deep breath on the phone and said, vulnerably, "This is hard."

"Yes," I agreed. "And wouldn't you rather know now, before you arrive and have a miserable week, or before you cancel and cause her to wonder what's going on with your friendship, or before you completely stress out for the next two weeks for no reason at all?"

One week later, I got a text that said, "It worked!" Her friend had been stressed about final exams and wanted to focus. They ended up having a blast on their vacation together. The right stories get the right results.

Checking in with someone to verify the truth of your story can be a fantastic step forward for making sure you don't go down the wrong path. Sometimes your story may have a great deal of truth to it. Perhaps your spouse *was* upset by the altercation and needed time to process all the angles of your exchange. Then again, maybe your spouse was distant due to a distraction at work that had nothing to do with your disagreement. It's also quite possible your spouse was simply coming down with a common cold, and now multiple wet sneezes are warning you that even more distance might be best for all. Checking in on the story in your head helps you more fully understand the pieces on the board and how to best move them so you can get what you want. (But you definitely don't want that cold.)

ANOTHER MAGICAL PHRASE FOR STEP 3: *HELP ME UNDERSTAND; WHAT'S THE THOUGHT BEHIND...?*

People do things that are sometimes truly unexplainable to you. They say something, have a facial expression, or behave in a way that is perplexing and that can make connection harder. Sometimes people say or do things that you immediately perceive as rude or inappropriate. Before you start making false assumptions about their intent and weaving a story that may have no basis in reality, ask them about *their* story.

Perhaps on a Friday night you're innocently sipping your cocktail and complaining about your stress levels with your friends when suddenly someone says something super snarky and, to be honest, a bit mean. Instead of escalating the situation in the moment and reacting with a "What the—?" you decide to wait (and let the alcohol wear off, if you think it might be an influencing factor) and address the situation after you've taken time to prepare for this conversation. On Sunday, you call your friend, and, after taking a moment to reconnect about everyone's weekend activities, you ask, "Hey, help me understand; what was the thought behind that remark Friday night?" The thought behind their words and actions often reveals their own unfulfilled want.

When appropriate, you don't need to wait. Sometimes the best time to address an off-putting comment is in the moment, but after you've taken a deep breath.

🧠 Hey, help me understand; what's the thought behind that comment?

can clear up any hurt or misunderstandings immediately so they don't fester. You're now leaning in instead of reaming them out or accusing them of body swapping with an alien.

Speaking of alien abductions, let's talk teens. While you know your son's enthusiastic age-eight personality will be returned to his body at some later—much later—stage of life, right now his age-fifteen pain-in-the-ass apathy and grunts are driving you crazy. A well-placed "Help me understand; what's the thought behind that grunt?" can lead to a constructive conversation and an unexpected opportunity for connection or simply a request for more cereal. Either way, you'll learn about his wants and get more than two words out of your teen. At this age, a complete sentence is often one of the things a parent wants. Don't expect more than ten words, though. Keep your expectations low, and you'll get more of what you want. Just keepin' it real. A teenager's mind is not fully developed. Mark Twain is often credited with saying, "At age fifteen, I could hardly stand to be around my folks because they were so dumb. When I turned twenty, I was surprised how much they had learned in five years." Keep the faith.

DON'T BE INSULTING (OR AN ASS)

One of the best things you can say to an upset person is: "Help me understand; what's the thought behind your tears?"

You make no false assumptions or incorrect interpretations about what might be taking place.

Judgmentally asking a man or woman what might be causing their behavior is never cool. Questions such as "Is it shark week?" or "Feel the need to participate in a pissing contest?" are insulting. Even if your intuition is right, these remarks are all shades of wrong. A simple, sincere "Help me understand; what's the thought behind...?" can turn a bad situation into a much better one, or at the very least a survivable one. Do not add any commentary other than stating the obvious. If you become even slightly judgey, it will backfire. "Help me understand; what's the thought behind your out of control rage?" "Help me understand; what's the thought behind your ridiculous rant?" or "Help me understand; what's the thought behind your incoherent babble?" will not get you anything you want in the foreseeable future.

When you truly do not understand someone's actions or words, instead of reacting, pause. Take a moment to respect that whatever they may be experiencing, at the crux of it is an unmet or unsatisfied want. Are they frustrated? Are they disappointed? Are they hurt? You won't know what tension, resistance, or blocks they're facing until you say: "Help me understand; what's the thought behind...?"

When you reach out and help others get what they need and want, you're left with a really good feeling. Feeling good about who you are and how you serve is a basic human want that perpetuates the upside of humanity. Be a good human, help others get what they need and want, and you may be surprised at how many people want to return the favor and give you what you want. Whether you believe in karma or not, being swept into the cycle of giving and receiving really helps you get whatever it is you want.

GET WHAT YOU WANT—WITHOUT HOOKING AN EGO

You can best manage and prevent Ego Hooks by acknowledging rather than ignoring the role of everyone's egos and how they might be triggered. Plan accordingly for these additional conversations and you (and your ego) are much more likely to get what you want.

I need to speak with: ....

Outcome I desire: ....

The story I currently have in my head about this scenario is...

....

....

....

What do I fear this situation might say about me?

....

....

....

What might the other person fear this conversation says about them?

....

....

....

What is true about each of our roles?

....

....

....

What is not?

....

....

....

What might I be missing about their perspective or story?

....

....

....

What might I be resisting or judging about this scenario?

....

....

....

How might I frame this conversation to reduce the likelihood of triggering their ego?

....

....

....

What might I say to assure them they are a good person, competent, respected, accepted, or loved?

....

....

....

Uncovering the stories of others is equally important. Gaining insight into their thoughts and stories will help you respect their perspective and honor their version of reality. It will also help you avoid hooking an ego. Knowing *how* they perceive their past, present, and future world helps you tremendously in creating an outcome they can believe in and support. The best way to do this is to ask them what they're thinking. Encourage them to share with two or three inquiries, such as:

- Help me understand; what's the thought behind your comment?
- How do you see/perceive this scenario?
- How are you seeing this play out?
- What might you be resisting or judging about this situation?
- What are you thinking might happen next?
- What are you hoping happens next?
- What are you hoping doesn't happen next?
- How are you envisioning this unfolding?
- How do you want this to unfold?

All parties believing in a shared next step is exponentially helpful for getting what you want.

So what happened with Coach? I wish I could tell you Sean and Leila had such a highly profitable conversation with him that he saw the error of his ways, apologized profusely, and awarded her Most Valuable Player for the season. Yeah, that didn't happen. Remember, the wand is *realistically* magical. Sean and Leila did meet with the athletic director and coach. They agreed on the team's many strengths, and they got aligned on their definitions of success on and off the court, all while managing to avoid triggering any egos in the process. But Coach was Coach and they didn't change his DNA. Coach was still a screamer, and he still favored his own daughter with tremendous amounts of playing time. The good news is that even though Coach still yelled at Leila, he yelled less, and never once did he again accuse her of almost costing them a game. Even better news, Tammy started attending every practice. Sometimes she arrived late, but she was there, running drills with her teammates. Coach seemed to get a little more fired up about running better practices, and Leila could tell that everyone on the team was taking the season more seriously. It paid off: they won league and first round of regionals, and the athletic director and Coach were helping her meet with colleges. Sean and Leila felt like this outcome was a solid victory, and Sean was enormously proud of his daughter for using her voice.

Not everyone will alter their stinky behaviors. Sometimes people need a more direct approach when you're asking them to modify their manner. The next time someone is all up in your grill and refusing to play better (and denying you what you want), it's time to call them on their shit. It's time for Step 4.

OWN YOUR SHIT AND DE-STINK THEIRS

Decades ago, when the business climate was different (but not different enough), a senior executive vice president of operations in a company I was consulting with was faced with an awkward conversation. Upon arriving at work one Monday morning, she learned that the company's VP of sales thought it would be a good idea to swim naked at a client's pool party over the weekend. In front of employees, independent contractors, and customers, he swan-dived into a pool of disrepute.

At first, the senior EVP assumed that this was an open and closed case. Swimming naked at a corporate event? Ask for resignation. But it was not that easy. Before she'd even had a chance to reheat her coffee, the company's CEO stopped by her office and politely informed her that while swimming naked was indeed not a great idea, it wasn't the end of this person's career. In fact, under his watch, the VP of sales was a sacred cow. "And," he continued, "please reprimand him before the day is over so that I can tell the client we've dealt with it."

While she was very tempted to react impulsively and judgmentally with her boss and say, "Are you kidding me?!" she knew it wouldn't help her cause or get her what she wanted. Oftentimes, removing the stink from the air requires a more strategic approach.

Instead, she took a deep breath and asked her CEO a series of questions so she could better understand how she might best address this challenge. "Can you please define 'reprimand' so I may better understand what you deem as reasonable consequences? What are we expecting in terms of his changed behaviors, and how much authority do I have to ensure commitment to these new expectations? How might we, as a company, respond to the client or to others who inquire as to our thought process?" And just for good measure and humor, she ended with, "Shall I buy him a Speedo or trunks for his next party appearance?" By inviting the CEO into the problem-solving process, she set herself up for greater success. These questions helped her define her boundaries with both managing up and managing down when she went to talk with her colleague.

Bearing the brunt of this awkward burden and unsure about how to handle the birthday-suit bather, she decided to do some heavy lifting prior to her tough conversation. She brainstormed a list of questions, including, but not limited to *How stupid are you? How do you expect the company to respond to your choices? How might we best rectify your actions? How much did you drink? If roles were reversed, how would you respond? Help me understand; what was the thought behind your action?* and *What are the possible unintended consequences we need to mitigate right now?*

She selected all but the stupidity and drinking questions (though tempting) for her meeting and felt more prepared than she had just moments prior. Armed and dangerous, she met him off-site for coffee and led with her opening question: "If roles were reversed, how would you respond?" He replied, "Knowing I just saw you naked, I think I'd be responding with a smile."

Time stood still. She felt her heart skip a beat in panic. Her mind raced. *How stupid are you? How stupid am I?! Did I really just ask that? Did he really just say that?! I am in over my head!* He just nailed her to her spot. *What an ass. WAIT! Deep breath. Wrong question. Score one slimy point for him,* she thought. *Questions do work; they just need to be the right ones. And I need to address his "stinky" behaviors and subsequent consequences more directly.*

Sitting up a little straighter, she responded with, "Not appropriate. But that seems to be your theme this week. How do you expect the company to respond to your choices? I'm not pleased. This was quite a choice. The client has called twice already, and I must return his call this afternoon. How are you expecting me to play this one out?"

This bathing behemoth of a bloke broke eye contact and shifted in his seat. His face reddened. After forty minutes, during which he did 90 percent of the talking and was starting to sound contrite, she concluded with her final question: "What can I count on you doing differently going forward?"

A terrific strategy for diffusing a stinky situation is to ask a question. A well-worded question can flip responsibility and change the course of a conversation. Too often you take on the burden of doing all the thinking and problem-solving when a well-placed question can put the onus back on the other person. Armed with thoughtful, open-ended questions, you can often get others to rethink their position. Once you've posed your question, you then need to actively listen and not be distracted by coming up with your next one. It's beneficial to you to have a few good questions tucked away in your back pocket. Asking a few solid, open-ended questions will help get the *other* person to shoulder responsibility for de-stinking their stench.

OWN YOUR STINK

Just about the time you're rolling your eyes at someone else's faux pas, the universe is sending one your way. Get ready to insert foot in mouth. We're all human. We've all done things or said things that pull us further away from what we want. We all have missteps we need to own up to; however, if your missteps are left unchecked, they can potentially move you further and further away from the life you desire. The sooner you accept that you may need to own your piece, the sooner everyone can accept theirs.

When it comes to de-stinking your slip-ups, keep it short and simple. "My bad. My fault. I own this one." Each one of these short remarks is a solid response for reducing tension. And when appropriate, apologize. Perhaps your colleague brings up your behavior in the prior day's meeting. You might need to say you're sorry with a line such as "Yesterday, I overreacted. I apologize." On the other hand, you may wish to simply acknowledge the blunder. "Yesterday, I overreacted. Today, I want to respond thoughtfully." You could also respond with, "You're right. I was upset yesterday. I apologize. I've thought it through, though, and here's what I think our next step should be..." Own your actions, take the stink out of the air, and decide if an apology is warranted.

Be careful not to apologize too often when a simple "Thank you for your patience," "Thank you for waiting," or "Excuse me" will suffice. Nonetheless, when an apology is deserved, offer one. Sincerely. Do not ruin your apology by beginning your remarks with a defensive explanation. For example, if your colleague calls you out regarding one of your not-so-hot moments and says, "You were late yesterday, and I'm tired of it," do not, under any circumstances, explain yourself as your first reaction. Your first response is to take the stink out of the air. Own your piece. Your best comeback is to acknowledge what's accurate and say, "I was late. I apologize." Only then might you add, "My kid started throwing up, and my morning got turned upside down."

Own your piece, and then move forward.

THE DE-STINK TECHNIQUE

When someone else is being "stinky" about your stink, one of the simplest, yet most effective, redirects for taking everyone's stink out of the air is none other than the De-stink Technique. This two-line method is perfect for when someone is bringing up an age-old gripe, harping on you, or nagging you about the same issue. Even if they are understandably upset about something that bothers them (e.g., not getting what they want), you can help dissolve the tension with the De-stink Technique while simultaneously helping both of you get what you want. This technique is brilliant for creating win-wins.

Getting what you want does not need to come at the expense of others not getting what they want.

First, identify and support their concern, which means laying down your defenses. Second, ask for help. That's it. A whopping two-line response. Super straightforward and, yet, it's a total redirect because you de-stink their issue while instantaneously aligning yourself with them as your ally in problem-solving.

Picture a woman sitting at the breakfast table sipping her coffee, lost in thought about her day, when her husband says, "For crying out loud, you threw lettuce away again!"

She looks up from her coffee, startled out of her reverie, and says, "Huh?"

Her hubby continues, "I'm looking at the trash. You threw away lettuce again! You do this every month. You buy more lettuce than we can use. It goes to waste, and we end up throwing it away. It's infuriating to me how much lettuce we waste."

A normal, human reaction would be to escalate this into a full-blown fight. She gets defensive, he gets more frustrated. The row becomes laden with judgment and disrespect. It starts to pivot toward poor money management and values misalignment, and ends with a rant on world hunger and why she can't get off her butt and send out two more résumés. Ahhh...see all the things this conversation might possibly be about other than slimy lettuce leaves?

But, armed with the De-stink Technique, this gal takes a whole new approach and implements the two-line method by waving her realistic magic wand. Instead of fueling the fury of her husband, she responds by saying, "Throwing away lettuce frustrates me too. Will you help me?"

Wait. What? Oh yes, it was so quick, so magical, you might have missed its brilliance.

Let's break down this magical response in slow motion. First, she identified his concern (throwing away lettuce). Second, she supported his concern by identifying and inserting his expressed emotion (frustration). Third, she added the words *me too*. Lastly, she asked the golden question: "Will you help me?" In other words, let's not vent, let's not argue, let's problem-solve together.

Her response could easily have been "Throwing away lettuce annoys me too" or "Throwing away lettuce upsets me too." Pick the emotion that best matches or aligns with the other person, and then implement line two by asking for help.

Warning—reality check here. The other person may lob one more hand grenade because the pin was already pulled, and they were preparing for battle. Side-step it if necessary. They may sputter some more, and you may have to say again, "It really does frustrate me too. Will you help me?" Implement these two simple sentences, and suddenly your bad habits and ruts and tough conversations start to shift, and you get closer to what you want.

A few more examples:

- Arriving late upsets me too. Will you help me?
- Food still stuck on the forks when unloading the dishwasher annoys me too. Will you help me?
- Running out of toilet paper frustrates me too. Will you help me?
- Always being too tired for sex disappoints me too. Will you help me?

The De-stink Technique is the perfect tool when you are being criticized or someone else is not getting what they want because of your "stinky" behaviors, even when the two of you view the severity of the situation differently. Instead of defending, blaming, pointing fingers, or refusing to admit that maybe, possibly, on a rare occasion, some of your habits are questionable to others, simply agree and align. It will help stop the argument or criticism in its tracks and help you both get more of what you want, which is less contention and confrontation and more compassion and connection.

BACK THE TRUCK UP

It works in reverse too. Imagine you're not getting what you want. Maybe your significant other does something that is mildly annoying to you today, but you know it will be driving you batshit crazy within two years unless you deal with it now. "You're a terrible driver" is not going to improve your partner's automotive skills nor get you endearing brownie points. Nor will "Are you blind? Your driving skills suck!" Yikes! The next time you want your partner to use a turn signal, go with the flow of traffic, or get a clue about how lane changes work, say nothing. Yep, you will wait and address their hazard to your safety later, when you are not in the car. Obviously, if they don't see the eighteen-wheeler, point it out, loudly, but do not criticize in the moment. Bite your lip and fasten your seat belt.

For those of you who are having a hard time not offering driving advice from the passenger seat, take heart. You're not avoiding the tough conversation. You're avoiding distracting the driver even further, and you're strategically preparing for what to say, when to say it, and how to say it. Maybe you two are out hiking in the woods or relaxing on the couch after dinner. When the mood is chillax, you can share, "I got scared today when you almost hit that car.

You got distracted, and it worries me. Is there anything I can do to help?"

There may be nothing you can do to help, my sage and savvy reader, and you will need to take solace that addressing the issue is *still* moving you closer to getting what you want, albeit a tad slower than you may appreciate. Then again, there might be something that your partner requests. The goal of this conversation is to signal to your partner that you care enough to offer. Note, too, that there are no absolutes or superlatives in the above de-stink example. Saying "You're always distracted" or "I'm petrified of driving with you" will not help. State one comment about one specific incident and offer to help.

Let's play this out one step further. The very next day, your partner is again distracted, and you literally slam your foot on the imaginary brake in front of you as the car comes to a screeching halt in heavy traffic. Do. Not. Say. A. Word. Later, when not in the car, get more direct. "Baby, today was another close call because, it seemed to me, you were distracted. It was more upsetting to me than yesterday. Is there anything I can do to help?" If your partner says no, then you respond with, "Okay, I've offered to help, and you have declined twice. Your safety matters to me. My safety matters to me. Do you understand my perspective? Is this making sense to you?"

If your partner says, "Yes, thank you," you may then ask, "What might we do to ensure our safety the next time we're riding together?"

If your partner says, "No," share a feeling. "I feel nervous when you're driving and distracted. Does that make sense?" If your partner says, "Yes," see above. If your partner says, "No," then it's time to set a boundary. One possibility may be "I'm going to take a break from riding with you until I feel it's safer." Your partner may feel unduly criticized. Your partner may think you are overreacting. Your partner may say, "Whatever." You cannot control your partner's reaction. What you can control is how you establish a boundary and position yourself to begin getting what you want—a safe journey. What you just did was beautifully connect the De-stink Technique with knowing where to draw a line. Now follow through. NEVER draw a line you're easily willing to erase, or all future lines will be meaningless and trodden over. Yep, that means you must find your own transportation and meet your partner at the next event. Download a transportation app or borrow your friend's bike if you have to, but, whatever you do, follow through. You'll never get what you want if you're wishy-washy when it comes to your own self-worth (and safety!).

STINKING FROM THE INSIDE OUT

Sometimes your own internal struggles will prevent you from getting what you want most. A coach once told me, "You get what you are." If you are someone who walks around having conversations in your head about not being worthy of your wants, you'll do everything to prove yourself right. Undermining, self-sabotaging, and ruining other people's wants as you simultaneously destroy any chances of getting your own are just a few classic behaviors of "Wanters" who feel worthless.

I don't deserve it is a self-limiting belief that encourages you to settle. Settling is the kiss of death. You literally start living a life of mediocrity you so don't want. You may struggle with self-limiting beliefs and thoughts such as:

- I'm not worthy of my wants.
- I'm not good enough to ask for this.
- I'm not smart enough to make that happen.
- I'm not creative enough to figure it out.
- I'm not talented enough to get it right.
- I'm not meant for more.
- I'm not allowed to ask.

Be open to using your wand on yourself by changing the internal conversations that hold you back. Challenging your limiting beliefs and dropping the stories that do not serve you well will be wildly powerful in expanding your possibility and getting the life you so very much want. When you're willing to change your thinking, you're then capable of changing your behaviors. When you're willing to change your actions, you are going to get a whole new result. That's just how it works, my sweet snickerdoodles.

In order to do this heavy lifting with your own internal dialogues and debates, you need to consider that much of life is make-believe. What you believe is just a story you tell yourself. Stories that self-sabotage or reinforce your own sense of lack or worthlessness are hard to rewrite, but they can absolutely be fully edited.

What narrative are you scripting? What false assumptions might you be making? What whoppers might you be telling yourself? The thoughts you have rumbling around in your head from prior experiences might be biased notions you hang on to with a ferocious grip to justify your stance and tactics, or they could be legitimate stories that helped you once successfully navigate the choppy seas of your life. Warning: the tactics that worked for you previously may no longer serve you well for the unchartered territory ahead. You might still be struggling with doubt, guilt, or shame derived from past behaviors or events. When you dig into your own thoughts, you'll figure out which of your beliefs are working for you and which ones are preventing you from getting what you long for most.

Challenge the roots of your beliefs and who passed them on to you. You didn't start making up stuff until someone started passing their stories (also known as their baggage and bullshit) on to you. Sure, some of the stories they told you were positive and affirming, and strengthened your sense of spirit and self-worth. Cheers and thanks to these affirming, mature adults who helped you develop a strong sense of self. They told you stories such as *Your voice matters. You're worthy of love. You're super creative. You're great at solving problems. You are so thoughtful and generous. You will accomplish anything you set your brilliant mind on achieving. I believe in you.*

Other stories you heard may have been intended to tear you down or keep you in your place, or were projections of someone else's own insecurities or bass-ackward thinking. Unfortunately, you were too young to understand or challenge their limiting, unconstructive beliefs. *You're not smart enough to do whatever you want. Who do you think you are? Money doesn't grow on trees. You're lazy. Hard work pays off. Your sister's the pretty one. Do not talk about yourself positively; it's boasting and unbecoming. Ain't nothing in life free. Follow your bliss, and you'll never work a day in your life. Nobody's going to take you seriously unless you have a PhD. If you swallow your gum, it will stay in your stomach for at least seven years.* Really? Really?!

Not every story in your head developed from someone

who spoke to you directly. You also picked up stories about how the world works and your role in it from the books you read, from the covers of magazines you looked at, and from watching the actions of others, to name a few sources. You still write stories and carry them around with you when you watch the news, stand in line at the store, or open your eyes and look around. If you're awake, you're crafting a narrative about something. You're hard-wired for story, and if your limiting stories go unchecked, they can be destructive.

If everywhere you go, you're often wondering, *What stinks about this situation?* you need to first check the stench emanating from within. Starting today, take responsibility for de-stinking your own internal shit so you can get what you want. No excuses.

WHERE YOU MIGHT GET STUCK

I met a woman last year whose picture may appear next to the word *miserable* in *Webster's Dictionary.* If you don't find her there, then you'll definitely see her in Booth Thirteen of the swap meet where they sell cheerless objects to embittered buyers under overcast skies. And it was a privilege. Yep, meeting martyrs and not-so-silent sufferers is a privilege. But...I don't want to meet them on a regular basis. Miserable martyrs (so aggrieved by their life that they are an occasional annoyance and very good lesson in yours) are best met every few years to serve as a wonderful reminder of who we don't want to become in this very short gift of life.

With eager anticipation and a bounce in our step, a friend of mine and I wove our way through the streets of Seattle. We were headed to meet his colleagues for dinner in a fabulous new restaurant getting rave reviews online. A part of me is a foodie who loves nothing better than to experience fine food and fine wine with even finer friends. I was stoked.

We walked in right on time, took our seats at a table that let us view the creative operations in the kitchen, and ordered a bottle of wine. I was feeling pure bliss when I looked up to see a couple making their way toward us. The gentleman waved and his wife scowled. Oh dear. *Someone is not a happy camper*, I thought. That was the understatement of the night. This woman did not want to be there. Nothing was satisfactory to her, nor was she going to allow even the faintest of smiles to cross her face. She was clearly under duress and only said yes to this soiree because her husband had asked her to attend. She did not wish to drink, she did not wish to eat, she did not wish to learn much about us. When I finally unearthed from her that she had a young son who played basketball, I thought, *Hallelujah, we have a connection.* I'm from a family who is passionate about basketball, and so I shared,

"Do you love going to your son's games? I love watching my niece and nephew play." Without missing a beat, she made fierce eye contact with me and said, "I do. I never miss his games. Until tonight."

D'oh! Well, that explained why she was acting like she had a corncob stuck up her butt all night. She did! She was pissed. She didn't get what she wanted. While we can all empathize with her feelings, I encourage you to not replicate her behavior.

You set the tone and tenor of your life. You choose how you show up. Check your energy at the door, my friends, and if your energy is lousy (aka stinky), then either change your attitude or change the direction of your feet and walk away. This woman—an adult, I remind you—had a choice. Don't go to dinner and go to your son's game, or go to dinner and don't be a twit about it and ruin ours.

A great technique when you feel like you are acquiescing to something you don't want to do is to say, "No, thank you." Shocker, I know. If you know something or someone is going to totally drain your energy or make you a miserable, stinky wretch, do everyone (most especially yourself) a favor, and decline. If you choose to do something because you know another person really wants you to do it, then channel your love for this person into your energy and enthusiasm. Show up with the thought *This may not be my first choice of activity, but my husband is my first choice in humans*, and make an effort to genuinely smile and connect. Saying yes to something you don't want to do and then being a wet blanket about it is simply boorish.

I accepted her basketball reveal as an opportunity to connect. She didn't want to be where she was, and, at the very least, I wanted a less painful evening. Focusing the rest of the night on her, we talked about her son, our shared love of basketball, and what a fine young man they were raising. Irrespective of how a series of events starts, you choose how it transpires. You write the scenes in your life, and you choose how you walk through them. You script the narrative of your wants.

A MAGICAL PHRASE FOR STEP 4: *AND YOU'RE SHARING THIS WITH ME IN THE HOPE THAT I DO WHAT?*

Whether you're dealing with a difficult person who's back in your office complaining or sulking again, or you're listening to someone tell you bizarre stories about your coworkers' bathroom habits, this magical phrase is for you.

"And you're sharing this information with me in the hope that I do what?"

A lot of people like to vent. They'll share information with you just to share. Other times, people are venting because they hope if they complain loud enough and whine often enough, you'll fix their stinky problem. It's important to inquire about their intentions and expectations of you. Instead of giving away your precious time just so they can pout, you ask: "And you're bringing this dilemma to me with the hope that I do what?"

Their venting cannot be tolerated, as your time and energy is way too precious.

Sometimes people share information with you because they have a hidden agenda. Perhaps you're dealing with a volunteer who believes he should be paid, and, for the ninth time, he's explaining to you why he's such an underappreciated asset. Maybe someone is in your office sharing gossip about another colleague. You're not sure why, so you ask, "What action are you hoping I take with this information?"

Turning the tables and inquiring about their expectations works beautifully. Instead of taking the complaint and accepting responsibility, you put the responsibility of thinking back on *them*. You stop the whining and shift the conversation to better understand their desires and outcomes. *What do they really want?* Seeking to understand someone, to dig a little deeper into their motives, is often eye-opening and constructive. When you better comprehend someone else's drivers, you can assist them in getting what they want or sometimes even redirect their desires by showing them how their words and actions are possibly working against them. Understanding others' intentions also enables you to get more of what you want by setting up win-win scenarios.

For example, a direct report of yours says something snarky in a meeting. Instead of escalating the situation, you privately invite him to your office after the meeting and ask, "What was the thought behind that remark?" You're now leaning in instead of reaming out. You're also in discovery mode. Asking, "What was the intention behind the remark?" helps you discover what he really wants. The more you learn about another, the more likely it is for you to capitalize on a solution that works for all, change an individual's or group's behavior, and co-create a better future.

Instead of accepting someone's complaint and therefore tacitly accepting the responsibility for taking action, ask, "And you're sharing this information with me in the hope that I do what?" When you ask this question, you put the responsibility of resolving the situation back on the difficult person. This magical response can easily be modified to:

- How are you hoping I respond to this information?
- What action are you hoping I take with this information?

Any one of these gems will stop the whining and shift the onus of doing something about it back to them. You're brilliantly setting boundaries around your time, energy, and efforts. These magical one-liners also shift the conversation so you may better understand the other person's desires and motives. What do *they* really want? Once you know what they're after, you'll be better able to respond appropriately. You may extend an offer or request that fulfills their need, you may end up offering an alternate but viable solution, or you might smile and say: "Not happening, but here's what is going to happen."

Then you clearly state what you want.

Colleagues complaining about one another at work is as commonplace as flies at a picnic. Both are annoying. The next time someone knocks on your door and says, "Do you have a minute?" and they follow this request with a ten-minute rant about how much they dislike Deb, there's only one initial response: "And you're sharing this information with me in the hope that I do what?"

They might want you to take action, they might not. They

might want *you* to speak with Deb. Here's your next response.

> I hear you. You sound (insert feeling word here such as concerned, upset, or frustrated). First, you need to address your concerns directly with Deb. If things don't improve after you speak with her, are you hoping we might all sit down together?

If they're hesitant to talk to Deb, you can coach them on the 5 Essential Steps, but it's important to not be a lawn-mower leader. Letting them address and take responsibility for solving their own problems will help them retain their power and build their confidence. Helping them to help themselves leads to a much better outcome.

WHEN YOU'RE NOT DONE WITH COMPASSION

The flip side of this magical phrase is an awesome way to make yourself useful and be a loyal ally at the same time. A family member, colleague, dear friend, or spouse shares something with you that reveals their vulnerability. They're stressed-out, anxious, or uncertain about what to do in response to a difficult scenario they are dealing with at work or with another person. Instead of jumping in to rescue them, and inadvertently insinuating that they can't rescue themselves, turn this magical phrase around and say:

- It means a lot to me that you shared this with me. How might I best support you? What do you need most from me right now?
- It means a lot to me that you shared this with me. As advice columnists frequently say, "I can't tell you what to do or say, but ask yourself, 'Am I better off doing or not doing this? Am I better off staying or going? Am I better off saying X or saying Y?'"
- How are you planning to respond?
- What are you thinking might be the best response?

They might be looking for a safe harbor to process it all, they might want your ideas or insights, or they might just want a hug. Asking them what they want from you is an awesome way to be the hero by granting them their wish. (I'm pretty sure, every now and then, you want to be someone's hero.) This approach creates a win-win on wants.

A CATEGORY 5 STORM OF STINK

Sue couldn't believe her ears. Not only was her three-year-old screaming at the top of his lungs in the middle of the store aisle, but Sue's mother (who was shopping with her) was criticizing Sue for her lack of parenting skills.

"I never let you kids behave like this," were the final words Sue heard from her mother as she picked her son's body off the floor, causing him to wail even louder in protest. A dozen curse words came to mind as she steeled her last nerve, ignored the stares from fellow shoppers, and headed straight outside to the car.

"Breathe," she said, attempting to calm her own nerves. Wishing she had a third arm, she managed to safely lock-hold her son against her torso as she searched for her car keys. As soon as she opened the rear door, her dearly beloved son arched his body in protest while simultaneously headbutting her in the chin. Sue saw stars. She didn't know whether she was going to cry, scream, or both. *What a shitshow of a day*, she raged internally, hoping she wasn't bleeding. She ignored her son's decibel-increasing shrieks as she snapped him into his car seat. She wanted him safe, first and foremost. She let him wail, noting out of the corner of her eye that her mother was approaching cautiously. Internally, she started counting backward from ten, letting her son scream a little longer. He was safe. She wasn't bleeding, just pissed and exhausted. She looked for his favorite snack in his backpack and found fish crackers, raisins, and a juice box. Not all was lost.

"Hey, Matt," she began. "You sound really upset. After you take a few deep breaths, I'll give you a hug or a snack and we can talk about it." She started taking deep breaths of her own. She looked up to see her mother shaking her head as she walked the last few feet to the car. She ignored her mother and turned toward her son. "Hey, Matt, are you more 'hangry' or more in need of a hug?" she asked, making herself smile. He turned his head away, dismissing her offer. *All moms are getting the cold shoulder today*, she thought.

"You shouldn't have stormed out," her mother chirped. "I read about temper tantrums online. Ruth in my grandparenting Facebook group sent me a link. It was written by a family therapist. He said don't leave. You're supposed to stay there and model calm."

Sue wanted to tell her mother where she could shove her Facebook group advice, but she knew that reacting with a temper tantrum of her own wasn't going to help, as tempting as it was.

"Mom, how are you hoping I respond to this advice? Clearly, I walked out. So how are you hoping to make me feel right now?"

Her mother's eyebrows lifted. "I...I was trying to be helpful. You clearly need help."

"You're right. Thank you, I do need help. The most helpful thing you could do for me right now would be to go back inside and grab a few basics. If I text you a few things, can you please go get them while I chat with Matthew?"

Her mother pursed her lips and then said, "If that's what you want."

"It is. Thank you, Mom. Thank you so much. I'm going to text you a few quick things right now." Sue made full eye contact with her mom. "Thanks, Mom, I know how much you love to help, and this is super helpful." With a quick text out of the way, Sue turned to her son, whose sobs were quieting.

Her mother's phone pinged. "I got your text," she said, awkwardly staring down at her phone. "I still think you should have stayed."

Sue looked up. Her patience was running thin. "Mom, I know you do. I heard you. Can we agree that I love Matt and my instinct was to get him calmed down and to a safe place?"

"Of course you love Matt. I love Matt too. I was—"

"I know, Mom, and I did my best in the moment. It may not be what I do next time or what a therapist thinks I should do, but can we agree I'm doing my very best and it may not always be right?"

"Of course. I...of course you are, dear...I...I'll be back as quick as I can."

"Want a fish or a raisin?" Sue asked, opening up the baggies as she turned to look at her son's puffy-eyed face. He silently stuck out his hand. "Hmmmm," she smiled. "I'm going to give you a fish first. If you don't want it, just leave your hand open and I'll take it back. If you do want it, you better quickly take it before I get to eat it." Humor would save her, and an aspirin.

Hours later, Sue was sharing her day with her husband as they prepped dinner.

"Sounds tough," he said, reaching over to kiss her on the forehead. "And it also sounds like you were amazingly calm."

"A part of me was so embarrassed and scared. He was inconsolable."

"Oh, baby, I get it. I wish I could have helped, but really, it sounds like you did everything right."

"I have this story in my head that I'm a terrible mother. That everyone in the store thinks I'm this terrible mother. My own mother thinks I'm a terrible mother."

"Well, that story sucks," he said. "And it's not even true. First, and most importantly, your mother doesn't think you're a terrible mother. She just believes that criticism, in all forms, is how you show someone you love them."

"She must love me a lot," Sue joked.

"She loves you tons," he laughed. "And as for everyone in the store, who gives a shit what they think? But, more likely than not, they were all recalling the time it happened to them. 'Cause it has."

"A part of me wants to go back and redo it," Sue said, picturing how it all unfolded and thinking about how she might have course corrected. "And a part of me hopes it just never happens again."

"Makes total sense."

"What I really want is an ice pack for my chin. Matthew's head is solid!"

"Coming right up," he said, turning toward the freezer. "Might it be time to talk to your mom too?"

Sue sighed. "I was hoping we could just move to Antarctica."

"I'd follow you *almost* anywhere," he teased. "And she makes a mean key lime pie. Can I show solidarity with you and still want her key lime?"

Sue smiled. "Maybe. Ugh. I know. It's time to set some new boundaries."

"I'm happy to help you walk through it. Starting with, *How might we...?*" he prompted.

"How might we..." Sue repeated. "How might we show each other more love and support, or wait, maybe, How might we create an even stronger mother-daughter relationship?"

"You got this," he said, dumping ice in a baggie.

"Hey, babe," Sue continued. "How might you respond if I opened a bottle of wine and asked you to show me how much you adore me?"

GET WHAT YOU WANT, SANS STINK

It's rarely too late to own your piece and apologize or to change the tone and tenor of an old pattern of interaction.

- What piece of this situation do I need to own?
- Might I need to offer up an apology first and foremost?

- If yes, an apology is needed, what will I say? If no, an apology is not needed, what might I say to acknowledge my piece?

Before you nag, harp on, or criticize another (aka get stinky), ask yourself,

- What am I really trying to get?
- How might I increase my odds of getting it if I seek connection?
- How might a new approach be more effective?

If your internal stories are so stinky they cause you to struggle with honoring, accepting, and fulfilling your own wants, take a moment to answer the following questions.

- What do I believe?
- Who or where did I get these beliefs from? Were these healthy and supportive sources at the time? Are they healthy and supportive sources now?
- Which of my beliefs are affirming and supportive of living the life I desire?
- Which of my stories, limiting beliefs, and negative thoughts may be preventing me from going after and getting what I want?
- Which of my stories may not even be true?
- What stories or negative thoughts might I need to drop?

- If I replaced these limiting beliefs and negative thoughts with more positive, forward-focused, affirming stories, who might I become and what might I create in my life?
- Who do I need to become, and what do I need to choose to believe about myself now to lead into what I really want?

Hitting the reset button with yourself or with others can quickly take the stink out of the air. Use your wand to freshen up your approach, and you'll be pleasantly surprised by how effective you are at moving things forward faster and getting what you want. After the first four steps, if you're still in need of another ideal one-liner or you need to draw a more definitive line in the sand, Step 5 will help you turn a tough conversation into a highly profitable one.

KNOW YOUR LINES—BOTH WHAT TO SAY AND WHERE TO DRAW 'EM

When I was thirteen, I got fired from my first job. For stealing. My schoolmate Josie and I worked in an old ladies' clothing store adjacent to the high school. We were both freshmen, but, as I was a year younger than Josie, my mom had to sign a permit enabling me to work.

I loved this job. I could walk over after school and tag merchandise, rearrange carousels of tops and bottoms by size, take deliveries, and ring up sales. There was almost nothing in this shop that I wanted, which made it an ideal choice for a first real job. I would be able to keep my paycheck. One Saturday, Josie was ringing up a sale when the cash drawer got stuck. She couldn't open it more than about an inch, which prevented her from making change. Betty, the store manager who worked with us, was in the back room unpacking new merchandise. Josie asked me what to do. I looked at the customer and asked if she would write a check, thinking we'd get the sale and deal with the drawer later. The woman was happy to do so, and left, bag in hand.

The moment the bells on the door stopped jingling from her departure, we both turned our attention to the drawer. Josie yanked on it as hard as she could, and it opened about another half inch. Progress! But not enough. Something was stuck. I peered inside but couldn't see a thing. I said to Josie, "There's gotta be something jammed back there. It's always worked before." I was working my way through possibilities—a broken spring, wadded up bills, a chipped off piece of wood—when Josie suggested that I try to squeeze my hand in to see if I could feel anything. As I was tiny, or at least tinier than she was, I thought this was a great idea.

There was enough space to get my hand and wrist inserted until my forearm stopped any further advancement. I flopped my hand from side to side, but I couldn't reach back far enough to find the culprit. The door to the shop jingled again as a new customer entered, and Josie left my side to go greet her. I was literally standing there with my hand in the till when Betty's voice rang out across the store, "AmyK!" I jumped, but my hand was still trapped in the drawer.

Throbbing in pain at being yanked up with no place to go, my hand tingled as Betty quickly swooped down upon me with her wrath. Descending ever closer, I finally wriggled my arm out and stood there. I knew exactly what it looked like. Upon her arrival at the front desk, she slammed the drawer closed with such force that it sprang back, opening fully and normally. I turned beet red. Why didn't I think of that? Just slam it with righteous indignation!

What might have been a few seconds seemed to stretch on interminably. My throat closed shut. My chest grew tight. My eyes started to water. Just yesterday, my English teacher had quoted, "Me thinks thou doth protest too much" to a kid caught cheating, and, no matter what he said, my teacher was convinced of his guilt. What luck did I have when I was caught red-handed? Betty dismissed me to the back room for the rest of the afternoon. Within five minutes of my arrival the very next day, the shop owner fired me. Her first words were, "I have to let you go. You know why, don't you?" And I nodded. Not because I was guilty, but because I believed that no matter what I said, she would never trust me. She would never believe me over Betty, and Betty was convinced of what she saw. My voice failed me.

At thirteen, I did not know how to frame a funny or wise response. I did not know how to persuasively articulate that Betty's eyes saw a truth that differed from my own. I did not know how to convincingly present my side of the story to the owner. Instead, I felt abandoned by a classmate that never spoke up, I felt betrayed by a miraculously working cash drawer, and I felt let down by my own lack of confidence and my complete incompetence to speak up for myself.

And what a great lesson. I can picture myself standing next to that misleading and diabolical drawer as if it were yesterday. Since thirteen, there have been more instances when I have reacted poorly, whether by staying silent or blurting something hurtful. Each time such an incident occurs, I learn how to respond better, and better responses get us closer to what we want.

YOUR REACTION DOESN'T DEFINE YOU, YOUR RESPONSE DOES

Experiencing a physical reaction in your body when you're involved in a tough scenario or conversation is normal. Having your throat constrict or your chest tighten is a natural response. It's a sign that you care or are invested in some meaningful way. Whatever is happening has emotionally triggered something in you that is connected to your beliefs, values, or identity. Whatever is happening—it matters.

It's also quite common to have an emotional response that's not super mature, yet is still understandable. You're human. You're allowed to react. You're allowed to be angry, sad, frustrated, stressed out, totally pissed off, envious...you get the idea. It's how we express these emotions that matters most.

Suppose your friend swings by and announces he just made Forty under Forty. He's being recognized and rewarded for his high-achieving, kick-ass self and all that he has accomplished at such an early age. You just turned forty-three. Nobody's ever given you a trophy. You *might* be a skosh envious. Pretty normal and quite understandable. Envy is a signal to you that you're missing or wanting something that you are not getting. Perhaps you want more affirmation and praise for all of your hard work and efforts, or you're feeling a little insecure and want to feel a stronger sense of self-worth. All relatable, all human.

The question is, how do you respond? Are you snarky and say, "That's a paid award program, right? I mean, you paid, or your company paid for you to be featured, right?"

To which everyone else starts thinking, *Ouch. Whoa. Down, boy. What just got triggered in you?* Your snarky response says far more about you than it does about your friend. What it's saying is that you're *reacting* primarily from a place of not getting what you want. Maybe you're not feeling good about yourself. Maybe you're not feeling worthy, respected, or affirmed. Your reaction creates the precise opposite outcome of what you so desperately want. No one wants to offer you the praise and affirmation you seek when you're acting like a jerk, and because you know better than to say such snarky things, you're suddenly feeling even worse about yourself. Consequently, you're now further away from what you wanted instead of closer.

Or you have an entirely different response. You pause, take a deep breath, and acknowledge to yourself that you're a little envious. You tell yourself you'll deal with yourself and your envy later. In doing so, you can now respond out loud with a supportive comment, such as "Dude! Congrats! First round is on me!" and begin teaching yourself how to better deal with envy. With this response you are positively affirming your friend's accomplishment, creating connection, and building a better relationship. Most likely, you're also feeling better about yourself because you responded maturely and magnanimously.

Let's admit it. Having a verbal reaction by saying something inappropriate, snarky, or downright inane is human. It happens to all of us, but it is also oh-so-not helpful. Luckily, it's easier to override than you may think. You *are* capable of biting your tongue or counting to six so you can pause before you open your mouth. Your verbal response *is* your choice. It's under your control. You can't always control your emotional or physical reaction, but you can choose your words.

Perhaps you're negotiating a deal, and the prospect calls you back with another request to lower the price. You're frustrated. Maybe even a little angry. You've already lowered the price twice. You might react and say something such as "Suzanne, come on, we've lowered it twice already. You're breaking me now. This is nuts. Your request is unreasonable."

Suzanne is not pleased. She was hoping for a dialogue, not your 'tude. From her perspective, she's suddenly wondering how you'll act once the deal is signed. She's now hesitating *more*, not less. Instead of your initial reaction, suppose you paused. Suppose this pause then allowed you to use your wand to shift away from your fear of losing the deal and away from your annoyance that it's taking longer than expected. Instead of expressing your irritation and weariness, you cast a much more magical spell by responding with "Hey, Suzanne, I'm glad you reached out. You sound frustrated. Help me understand what's going on. Please say more about the thought behind this request."

This thoughtful response turns a tough conversation into

a profitable one. You sincerely want to learn more. You're not shutting her down, you're not afraid of her push-back, and you're introducing an opportunity for you to re-establish value in your product. A thoughtful response is going to get you much closer to a signed deal, which is exactly what you want.

LAUGHTER CAN BE LOVELY

Years ago, I was part of a senior management team, and we were negotiating a new salary package and bonus for a regional president (RP) when the CEO and RP reached a stalemate. There was awkward silence for about five seconds, and we all know how long five seconds can be when you can cut the tension in the air with a knife. All of a sudden, the RP looked up and said, "All I ask is for the chance to prove that lots of money can't make me happy."

Everyone laughed. The conversation was back on track, and the salary negotiations were finalized. The RP got what he wanted, and, as I later found out, even a little bit more than he'd anticipated. Proven one-liners can be magically helpful and needed. You may not be as funny as a stand-up comedian, but when you've got a brilliant one-liner in your back pocket, you are far more confident and competent in successfully handling tough moments.

Humor can defuse tension and work really well for helping you get what you want, as long as it's self-deprecating, unifying, and never at someone's expense. Understandably, in a personal relationship, you and your spouse may joke at the expense of a difficult family member behind closed doors, or at a friend's quirks or a kid's antics. Finding humor and sharing that humor can help you keep your sanity. It's a natural way to bond, relieve tension, and get validation that you're not the one that's losing your mind. However, in a professional setting, do not joke at anyone's expense. It's detrimental to all. Full stop. Don't do it. All of this precaution duly noted, humor at work that is self-deprecating or unifying can be brilliant.

Having a few good lines stored away in your back pocket will come in handy so you can avoid the disappointing scenario of thinking of the perfect retort too late—often hours later at a bar or right before you fall asleep. French philosopher Denis Diderot coined the famous phrase *l'esprit de l'escalier*, meaning "staircase wit." As the story goes, Diderot was so flustered by an argument at a party that he stomped away, only to think of the perfectly witty response once he arrived at the bottom of the stairs. Being armed and ready with some wise and funny responses will serve you well.

AN INSIDE JOKE

Last year, a friend and I were drinking wine and venting about life when his attitude abruptly changed. (A possible side effect of the wine.) "Let's stop venting and start meditating," he exclaimed. There was so much enthusiasm behind his suggestion, I didn't have the heart to tell him this invention of his had been around for a while. With drink in one hand and his iPad in the other, he started searching for beginning meditation videos we could watch and follow. It didn't take but a minute to land on one with over two million views. He set down our glasses and pressed play. The sound of ocean waves crashing onshore washed over us. A flute joined in. We closed our eyes and imagined all our stress and tension dissipating instantly.

Our instructor joined us, his words asking me to...to...I tilted my head. More words were spoken. I opened my left eye. My friend's eyes were closed. Okay, I needed to try again. I leaned closer to the iPad. A crick in my lower back reminded me I was not relaxed, but precariously perched on the edge of the couch. I closed my eyes and attempted to listen very carefully. Elmer Fudd's *Shhh, I'm hunting wabbits* raced across my mind from out of nowhere. (A possible side effect of my wine.) Our instructor continued, encouraging us to...to...good grief! I couldn't understand a word he was saying. I opened both of my eyes. My friend was grabbing his glass.

"I don't understand a word he's saying," he said, beating me to the punch. "Did you understand any of it?"

I shook my head. "It sounded like he was saying—"

"Suck, shit, banana," my friend interrupted, finishing my sentence. "Suck. Shit. Banana. That's what he was telling us to do. Breathe in. Breathe out. Say: 'Suck. Shit. Banana.'" I laughed so hard, I almost fell off the couch.

To this day, when a series of events goes askew or something isn't playing out the way either one of us intended, all we have to do is say, "Suck. Shit. Banana." This line, with its shared amusement, instantly reduces our tension and rechannels our frustration into a more relaxed and productive mode of conversing.

Your "inside joke" is a line you can use to get yourself or another back on track. Yes, there may currently be tension between the two of you or with life in general, but recalling the line is a humorous reminder that you aren't taking yourself or life too seriously. Inside jokes are fabulous spells your wand can cast easily to reset the tone, tenor, and direction of a tough conversation.

OFFERS AND REQUESTS ARE GREAT CLOSERS

You're never going to get what you want unless you incite

action. With any critical conversation, it's important to sustain the momentum so you don't find yourself in the exact same scenario six months down the road. Offering or requesting something for yourself or from others is one of the best ways to create and sustain momentum, expand future possibilities, and get that which you desire. It works in reverse too. Accepting help when offered is a great way to build connection. Most people want to be helpful, want to feel needed, and desire to serve. Repeatedly turning down sincere offers of help is not, well, all that helpful. For anyone.

Each offer or request that you make needs to be genuine and communicated clearly and directly. Too often you pad your requests or offerings with added hemming and hawing or unnecessary apologies leading up to the ask. You beat around the bush or you sabotage your own request with fifty thousand words when five will suffice. A straightforward proposition yields the best results. Get clear on the actions needed by either party to get you your desired outcome. Possible offers and requests might be:

- Offering grace
- Requesting an apology
- Offering an idea
- Requesting a new behavior
- Offering resources or support
- Requesting a new deadline or agreement

Your offers and requests must also be sincere, not manipulative. While we can all play on others' emotions or deploy devious tactics to manage a situation in a sneaky fashion, it's so not how the game is best played for long-term gain. Besides, it's unscrupulous and immature. Recently, I observed a teenage daughter manipulate her father. She used her baby voice, called him Daddy, and after eleven minutes of arguing her case and whining her way through all the reasons why she needed him to say yes, he relented. She was given exactly what she wanted. She left for her evening activities with her friends in a state of ignorant bliss. It was short-lived. The following day when she started all over again with a new want, a new whine, and two new requests for more money and a ride, everything backfired. She lost her allowance, was grounded, and her father told her he was tired of being manipulated. A cautionary tale that when we seek our wants through manipulative means, the outcomes are not always pretty.

Our offers and requests must derive from a place of honesty, genuine desire, and respect. Whether it's respect for ourselves, others, or both, hold your head high. Focus on getting what you want while respecting the dignity of all involved. You can absolutely use your magical wand to cast a spell over another by appropriately smiling, expressing confidence, or exuding compassion when you ask or offer something. Lastly, take the time to craft an action item that has value for all. Moving everyone toward their desires is exponentially beneficial.

THE POWER OF PAUSE

Once your offer or request has been made, take an oath of silence. Yes, silence can be deadly. It can also get you exactly what you want. The moment you make your offer or request—pause. Like the well-trained pooch down the street, simply stay. Not one more word, not one more gesture; just stay quiet. When you hush, my sweet petunia, and channel Simon and Garfunkel, you'll be amazed at how the sounds of silence are a segue delivering to you that which you just expressed as your longing.

Your silence makes space for possibility. You are opening up opportunities for people to consider their options, weigh their own wants, calculate the consequences, check in with their feelings, and even burp if needed. Hey, it's making space for the more important stuff. If you rush them, if you follow your ask with more explaining, rationalizing, or whining, you'll likely curb their enthusiasm for making your wishes come true.

Following your offer or request with silence is a beautiful one-two step. Your silence is an assumptive close. Grant this person the opportunity to accept help from you or do something to help you, and then wait to see how they respond. They may need some space to come to the same conclusion you already came to, which is that you should absolutely be given what you want because giving you what you want will help them get what they want.

Inversely, if you're making an offer and you follow your offer with silence, you're giving someone the grace of accepting your help, support, or apology without unnecessary awkwardness. Sometimes when you offer to help, you unknowingly contribute to their embarrassment or spark a lower sense of self-worth because, while you want to appear supportive and empathic, you didn't prepare for the conversation and you sound arrogant, condescending, judgmental, or holier-than-thou. Unintentionally, you say too much or you say the wrong thing and it hurts instead of helping. While it wasn't your intention, you still must own it. Preparing an offer ahead of time and thinking through your word choice can help honor the dignity of another. The simpler and cleaner you make your offers and requests, the easier it is for others to accept them.

Just a few years back, a dear friend of mine found her sweetheart later in life and they celebrated their love in marriage. He came with two children and an immature ex-wife whose primary goal was to be friends with her children instead of being their parent. Did I forget to mention his ex-wife cheated on him? Now, of course, it takes two to tango, but I share all this drama because it messily spilled into the neat and tidy life of my pal.

Surprising no one, these kids started to rebel. As their mom's guilt about being a major cause of the break-up of her family ratcheted up, it became easier and easier for the kids to manipulate her. She wanted to be liked and to be seen as the good one, so she started giving the kids anything they wanted. It also became easier for them to play one parent against the other. This ex-wife made my pal's new husband look like the worst father on the planet simply because he wanted his kids to follow a few rules and grow up to be responsible adults. I watched from the sidelines for years, sympathizing, listening, asking questions, witnessing it in real time, until one day my friend frustratingly shared that the oldest kid was beginning to talk to her as if she were an idiot. She said it was like he was channeling his mother. He was totally condescending, dismissive, and rude. I could picture it a little too easily. I stepped from the sidelines onto the field.

I encouraged my friend to nip his nastiness toward her in the bud. She need not be dragged into the drama, nor let the drama overtly influence her own sense of self. It was time to get what she wanted—a little respect. It was time for her to have a needed and overdue conversation and be clear about what was and was not cool about the kids' interactions with her. This was a prime time to make an offer and a request directly to the children, but only after first meeting with her hubby to get his buy-in and support with her strategy. Once they were aligned, she could meet with the kids one-on-one and lay out her boundaries.

Understandably, and reason number 4,782 why she loved her hubby, he supported her 100 percent. The following week, she met with each kid individually, starting with the oldest. She started off by sharing how much she enjoyed having dinner with him and going to his after-school games. All true and not over-embellished. She specifically praised him on a trait he possessed and she admired. She expressed her excitement in seeing him pursue activities and interests he enjoyed. She then made her offer and request. First, she offered not to be another parent. He certainly didn't need one more person telling him what to do. Not shockingly, there was no pushback from him. Second, she requested that he not speak rudely to her. As an independent adult, she was requesting that he recognize her role as simply another caring adult in his life and respect her boundaries. He wouldn't talk to his friends' moms the way he was currently speaking to her, and she expected that same kind of interaction. When she was done speaking, she purposefully paused and waited. He gave her a look filled with petulant teenage annoyance. She waited. She had mastered the art of the pause and was not about to dilute her stance with unnecessary filler. His lip curled, and when her expression still did not waiver, he broke eye contact and turned slightly away. Still she waited. With head bowed, he finally nodded. It was an important mini-win for her and a growth opportunity for him.

PREP, PRACTICE, AND ROLE-PLAY

When you prepare and practice for a tough conversation, you're accepting responsibility for your life. You're accepting the assignment you were given to care for and manage yourself.

A critical conversation with another person requires the same degree of planning as, say, taking a trip. Most people I know *really* benefit from purchasing their plane ticket ahead of time, making a hotel reservation in advance, and having some sense of their itinerary. This doesn't mean there isn't room for spontaneity and some zigging and zagging when you arrive. It just means you're *not* winging it and left stranded in some foreign city with no place to sleep, none of the right currency, and a dead cell phone.

If you want to have a profitable conversation and get what you want, one of the best ways to prepare is to role-play. Be the script writer, play the various parts, and direct. You don't literally need to act it out, but you might want to at least perform a casual role-play in your mind. Fight back a little. Throw yourself some shade. Blindside yourself with possible responses. Rehearse in front of your bathroom mirror. If those options aren't comfortable for you, then at the very least, curl up on your couch, close your eyes, and play the scene out. Walking through various scenarios in your head helps you develop well-constructed, strategic responses. It can also prevent you from saying or doing something that places you in a new scene you were hoping to avoid.

Picturing the scene on a movie screen and playing a friendly devil's advocate director will help you plan your moves, find your mark, and deliver your lines in one take. Which is good, because in real life, you get exactly one take for your upcoming conversation. Naturally, life happens. You might blow your lines, miss your cues, and need to do it all over again tomorrow, but it's not the same conversation. It's the second conversation. You're starring in a reality show that's "taped" before a live audience. You do not get multiple takes and a post-production editing team.

For the love of all things dark chocolate, do not wing the tough, critical conversations. Do not just say to yourself, *I'm a pretty good communicator, I can just wing asking for this raise. I can just loosely navigate this conversation with my in-laws and their lack of boundaries. I can just tell my partner that our sex life stinks.* Yeah, that'll go over well. The most important conversations in our life require respect for our wants and the wants of others, and we show respect by preparing.

Jumping into a conversation without preparation because you are emotionally triggered or taking on someone else's sense of urgency can lead to misspeaks, missteps, and misfires. If someone is knocking at your door and insisting you participate in hearing their want, you can certainly entertain their input, but you don't have to make a decision or take any type of action in that same conversation. You can say: "This is clearly important to you. I need some time to think this through."

Then take the time you need to strategize your response. Conversely, if you are rushing to get a decision from someone else or to "air things out" and you want the conversation to end profitably, curb your impatience and at least take a few minutes to prepare your framing and flow.

Sometimes your snarkiness can get the best of you. What's clever and funny in the moment may sound immature and petty as time goes by. Even if you think it's hilarious at the time, if the key phrase or question you verbalized comes back to haunt you, it will undo all the good you've done.

Once, I was on a boating excursion in Cabo when I heard a mother ask her miserable-looking teenage son, "Are you having fun?" "Yes," he replied. She responded, "Well then, communicate it to your face." I, along with several other adults, laughed internally all day long because it was funny in the moment. I can almost guarantee the young man found it a lot less amusing.

WHERE YOU MIGHT GET STUCK—LINES

It's important to keep in mind that your responses will either *hurt* or *help*. That's it. These are the only two options you get. There's no such thing as neutral. Whether it's a daily grind conversation with someone about buying toilet paper or a high-stakes critical conversation such as buying a house, everything you say will *hurt* or *help*. Your responses will chart the course of the conversation and determine how it ends and whether or not you get what you want.

Imagine you're racing out of the office. You're late. Tonight's date night. You've already texted your wife that you're twenty minutes away from home, but it's looking more like thirty minutes. Just as you merge onto the freeway, you sort of recall being out of toilet paper. You're pretty sure you used up the last roll this morning, but you're not certain. Now you're wondering if you should swing by the grocery store and grab some, but it'll delay you another fifteen minutes.

Your blood pressure starts to increase at the thought of

being more than forty-five minutes late for date night and seeing your wife's oh-so-not-pleased expression when you finally do walk through the door. Your own level of irritation starts to rise. Your thoughts start racing. Your wife is terrible about stocking up on things like tissues and toilet paper. It's annoying, to be honest. You were raised by a mom that believed a six-month supply should be on hand at all times, and your wife believes that an extra roll of TP lying around makes you a hoarder.

Do you call your wife and ask her to check, or do you not call? Do you just stop at the store and risk being ridiculously late for date night? Could you go without toilet paper? You picture yourself sitting on your throne tomorrow morning sans TP. Not good. So you call your wife and blurt out, "Hey, this is getting ridiculous; we should be stocking toilet paper—never mind—are we out? Do I need to stop and grab some?"

Uh oh. Upon hearing your irritation, and being irritated already with your lack of respect for date night, she reacts with, "How am I supposed to know? I worked all morning, the kids have been at me all afternoon, and I haven't even had time to poop once today, Mr. 'I poop three times a day.' "

Not surprisingly, instead of leaning in to listen compassionately, you react to her snarkiness with further snarkiness of your own. The conflict has now escalated, and by the time you get home, no one is in the mood for date night, and no one will be getting what they want.

What might have been a funny or seemingly innocent conversation about the need for more toilet paper instead created more friction, tension, and hurt. All because you reacted...out of instinct and bad habits. These conversational bad habits often create undesirable outcomes. When you line up all the repeated hurtful tones and tenors over the weeks, the months, the years, it isn't just one time, one conversation that led to one lousy date night. It's a series of unprofitable conversations that result in a really crappy relationship. Pun intended.

Does this scenario sound exaggerated? Maybe, but it happened. I've known couples who divorced over small differences such as toothpaste tube usage, unsecured juice bottle lids, and thermostat settings. Our words, our tone, our tenor—even when it comes to the seemingly mundane conversations of daily living, including buying groceries and picking up dry cleaning—impact the quality of our lives. Lousy conversations have even greater impact when it comes to the more significant decisions we make.

Suppose you and your spouse are getting ready to buy your first home together. Your words matter even more because you're either helping or hurting a noteworthy decision. Reactionary comments such as the following make a person feel defensive and disconnected. "Why is that floorplan so important to you? We don't need four bedrooms." "Why do you need this much backyard? I don't want that kind of water bill!" Remarks that are only about your wants, your needs, your perspective, and your judgments can escalate the stressors and anxieties that are already present in both people in tough decision-making conversations. In high-stakes conversations such as discussing buying a home, responses such as "Tell me more. Share with me the thought behind looking at four bedrooms. I know it's tough to balance budget and wants. It's tough for me too," reduce fear and increase understanding and connectivity.

For critical or highly sensitive conversations, I'll go so far as to put each of the words HURT and HELP in front of me on cards or Post-it notes, or leave my notes app open on my phone where I can see this beneficial reminder. The first words out of your mouth establish the tone and tenor of your conversations. Before you react, count to six using the one one thousand, two one thousand methodology, and by the time you're done counting, you will be much more likely to respond thoughtfully than to blurt out words you'll later regret. Thoughtful responses vastly improve the odds that you'll get what you want.

YOU DON'T HAVE TO BE A PROFESSIONAL ARTIST TO DRAW BOUNDARIES

In addition to having some solid lines at the ready, knowing how to draw a few good lines in the sand will also be quite beneficial to you. Drawing boundaries is an essential skill for getting what you want. The more you practice, the better you get.

Tough conversations only get easier when you have a strong sense of self and self-worth. When you have clarity on where another person's space ends and where your sense of self begins, establishing boundaries gets a whole lot easier. A US Supreme Court justice once famously said that your right to swing your fist ends at my nose. A lack of boundaries is self-sabotage, and your inability to draw them will seriously obstruct you from getting your heart's desires. Let's start with a basic technique for drawing a line in the sand that also incorporates a golden one-liner. A brilliant, fundamental phrase with three simple words is *No, thank you*. Why is this phrase so hard for some of us to say?! All you people pleasers, all you go-along to-get-alongers, I get it. I relate. Saying no can be difficult. YET, when you get clear on what you're actually saying *yes* to, it gets a whole lot easier. Saying no does not require an explanation, nor does it require an apology, but it does require clarity. This clarity comes from knowing exactly what you're saying yes to.

The next time someone asks, "Will you volunteer for this

committee?" take a moment to pause and think through what you really want. Before you utter a single, solitary word, and before they pounce on you, ask yourself, *If I don't want to volunteer, what am I saying yes to?*

Maybe by saying no to the volunteering, you are saying yes to more hours with your kids or more time to exercise. You might possibly be saying yes to less stress and more energy to complete an important project. Perhaps you're saying yes to some sorely needed time to unwind. Once you get clear on the yes behind the no, it's much easier to say it without apologizing, delaying a commitment that you don't ever want to fulfill, or saying yes resentfully. Martyrdom will not get you what you want, but it will give you hemorrhoids.

Imagine the next time someone says, "Can you do this for free? It'll be great exposure for you," you don't immediately acquiesce. Instead of saying yes, you envision yourself confidently saying, "No, thank you," or saying, "In order to share my services, I'll need X in return." If you really aren't interested in having your services or products exploited, stop and ask yourself, *If I don't want to volunteer my time or services for free, what am I saying yes to? My self-respect? My integrity? Investing my time in a better opportunity? Ensuring my value?* Getting clarity on what you're saying yes to is crucial for increasing your confidence and saying no with conviction.

WHERE YOU MIGHT GET STUCK–BOUNDARIES

Setting boundaries doesn't always require a verbal no. It can be a quiet, internal awareness of your limits and limitations and your own unique operating system. What you need and want to best manage an optimal, highly functioning you is exclusive to you. Do you know how to set limits with others as well as yourself? Do you know when to say yes and when to say no to yourself? Knowing *when* to say no is not the same as *being able* to say no. Fully knowing that we are separate from others helps us honor our own individual needs. It also makes it easier to filter out all the noise and take care of yourself. Can you hear your own needs and desires above the din of family, friends, neighbors, online posts, advertising campaigns, and well-intentioned soul-suckers? Can you feel your desires and needs through the screen of guilt, fear, or wanting to be liked? Setting boundaries is accepting the assignment of managing and caring for your own well-being. You are 100 percent responsible for your choices, decisions, and actions. When you can't say no to the requests, demands, and pressures of others, you are no longer practicing self-care but other-care. When you can't say yes to the self-care you need, such as time to refuel, reset, or rest, you've stopped accepting responsibility for self-love.

When you feel guilty because you believe you *should* say yes, *should* agree, *should* help out, you're no longer in self-control and self-management, but rather self-denial, and in some cases self-abuse. You tell yourself, *A good person helps. David needs me. Jane shouldn't do this alone. I'll sleep when I'm dead.* Even when you perceive that you are sacrificing your wants for the wants of others, it doesn't necessarily make you generous or a responsible adult. However, it can make you question why you aren't happier or why you feel empty or unfulfilled. It can make you wonder why you often feel lonely and left out or underappreciated and disrespected. It can result in your being stretched too thin or feeling plain ole over it and exhausted. Until you start to see that so-and-so isn't actually making you do anything without your willing consent, you will never practice the discipline of self-care and self-love. Learning to draw lines in the sand is a fundamental skill of getting what you want. It doesn't mean you never help others. It means that you take care of yourself so that you, as your most awesome self, can go out and make a positive difference.

Setting a boundary is not about building some huge, impenetrable wall. It's about installing a gate. You can walk through it when you want. You can come and go as you please. With a gate, you can easily hand out the security code to a few folks and you can deny it to others. If need be, you can change the code. In other words, there are times you will say yes. There are times you will step up, not out of resentful obligation, but because you genuinely want to lend a hand. There are times you will focus on yourself, without guilt, without fear, and without worrying that somehow you will be punished for prioritizing self-love. Taking care of yourself, showing yourself that you matter, and working through your resistance to setting boundaries is a splendid way to help yourself get whatever you want.

You may be thinking, *That's great, but what if they don't cave so easily? What if they snarl and bite and say horrible things in reaction to my offer or request?* Let them. Inoculate yourself against their choices. You're not responsible for their reactions. You are responsible for creating the life you want. One hundred percent responsible. The next time they throw a temper tantrum or behave egregiously, you might say in response to their tantrum, "Thank you for validating my request. As we can both see, it's more than understandable." Warning: this response won't have them sitting up, smiling, and waiting for you to toss them a treat and say, "Good boy!" What it will do is let them know you respect yourself enough to have boundaries, and you won't tolerate being pulled into their shitshow and being treated like poop.

A MAGICAL PHRASE FOR STEP 5: *WHAT HAPPENS WHEN...?*

There are times when people are clue-free about how their actions influence and impact others. When you need someone to modify their behavior and think it's their own great idea, this magical line is for you: "What happens when..."

This phrase is the perfect starter to a repercussion question. When you ask a repercussion question, you are helping whomever you're talking to draw their own conclusion about the consequences of a current situation they wish to avoid. As a result of these consequences they wish to avoid, you're also encouraging them, of their own accord, to make a decision to change the outcome, which—surprise—is the outcome you want.

Just last November, I was speaking at a conference when a woman came up to me after my presentation and asked, "AmyK? If I have a boss that won't give me the time of day, what would you suggest I do?"

"What's going on?" I asked. "I need a bit more context."

"He ignores me," she continued. "He won't give me feedback. He won't give me five minutes of his time, unless I screw up. Then I never hear the end of it." She shared that she is his administrative assistant, and he can't be bothered to talk to her unless there is a glitch in his schedule. She admitted that about once a quarter there is some type of scheduling snafu, and then he'll simply yell at her. All day long.

"Any suggestions?" she asked.

Now, you and I can both see there's a boatload of issues going on here, from accepting his tirades, to not establishing her boundaries, to why on earth she continues to work for a boss that won't talk to her. All not cool. However, since you and I don't have any context to her extenuating circumstances or constraints, let's refrain from being judgey and simply loan her a wand.

First, I asked her, "What do you want?"

She said she wanted a weekly five-minute meeting to ensure everything was set up perfectly and ready to go for him. Then I asked her, "What do you think your boss wants?" She was pretty sure he wanted a perfect calendar with zero conflicts.

That's when I shared that she needed to implement the magic of: "What happens when..."

I encouraged her to ask him, "What happens when your schedule is double-booked? What happens when there's a scheduling conflict?" The goal with this type of repercussion question is to have her boss envision a scene in a movie he doesn't want to star in. Let him feel the frustration. Perhaps he responds with, "I get angry. It's unacceptable. I look foolish to my clients, and it takes days to get the appointment back on the calendar, which delays everything."

I then suggested she respond to his answer with, "I want to avoid this frustration for you too. This is why it's so important to me to meet with you for five minutes once a week. Five minutes can all but guarantee this type of calendar conflict never happens."

The *What happens when...* question allows a person to visualize and articulate a problem and pain point they want to avoid. They'll consciously be more engaged once they've verbalized their pain, because they'll wish to bypass this awful outcome. As do you. Once they've articulated their pain, you can articulate the solution you desire that will alleviate their pain and get you both whatever you want.

This phrase also works beautifully when listening to your friends who want your compassion when they vent (or whine) but not your solutions. You still want to be helpful, and you'd prefer not to hear about this issue again next month. You might ask, "What happens when you don't stick up for yourself?" You have not offered a solution, you are not fixing their frustrations, but you are helping your friends to help themselves. When they see how their unaddressed issue plays out from their own actions, or inactions, and contributes to the pain they wish to avoid, you are helping them to formulate a strategy. You are helping them gather their courage, gird their loins, and solve their own dilemma. Voilà—you both get what you want, and you get the bonus of being perceived as an extraordinary listener and empathizer.

Last but not least, this is a magical phrase for parents everywhere.

- What happens when you forget your permission slip?
- What happens when you don't study?
- What happens when you forget to take out the trash?
- What happens when you don't ask for permission first?

These repercussion questions are lifesavers for parents who are tired of nagging and still want behavioral change. As I am a huge fan of positive reinforcement, remember to point out their awesome attitude and adjusted actions once they've given you exactly what you want.

SOLD!

What happens when... is a powerfully effective phrase in sales, too, because you are reminding your prospect of the pain that they wish to avoid and that *you* are about to resolve. In sales, every one of your prospects has pain points, and they can easily imagine the negative outcomes if they don't solve their problem soon. Asking the

What happens when... question at the beginning of your sales process is a brilliant way to address your prospect's biggest issues head-on.

- What happens when students fall behind?
- What happens when this valve leaks?
- What happens when your sales team misses its quota?
- What happens when you run out of storage?
- What happens when you miss filing the right legal forms?

No matter what product or service you sell, asking the *What happens when...* question about the problem you solve creates a solid framework in an initial sales conversation. It's a less pushy and pitchy way to explore the pain of the consequences and costs of their unaddressed problem, and it's a brilliant question to help you close more deals. If you're in sales, this is exactly what you want.

LOOK IN THE MIRROR

What happens when... is a great question to ask yourself. It can help motivate you to take action.

- What happens when I show up late to this meeting?
- What happens when I allow my boss to yell at me and disrespect me?
- What happens when I don't meet my deadline?

- What happens when I don't follow through?
- What happens when I say something too snarky?
- What happens when I don't turn in my expense report on time?
- What happens when I pretend to listen?
- What happens when I don't prioritize self-care?
- What happens when I don't draw a boundary?
- What happens when I don't speak up?

Motivation is not something you sit around and wait for, despite what you've been told. Waiting for a moment to "move you" is going to lead to a long wait. When you ask yourself, *What happens when...* and you play out the consequences and unintended consequences you'd very much like to avoid, you will be inspired to get off your derriere. Taking action *toward* getting the outcome you really want helps enormously *for* getting you what you want. It's not rocket science, but it is magical.

WHAT HAPPENS WHEN YOU USE YOUR WORDS

Peter was so annoyed with his brother Eric last month that he slammed the front door in his face. He was sick of being used. His brother pushed and pushed and pushed. Peter texted his buddy Kevin, and they met on the running path in the park. Jogging as fast as they could while Peter spewed his frustration, Kevin served as a silent sounding board.

Peter railed, "How could he? How could he even pretend this was okay on any level? I'm not okay with this. What was he thinking?"

Kevin grunted his support, his lungs pounding in protest at the pace. Peter finally slowed, his own chest laboring, and asked, "This is nuts, right? He should stop this craziness, right?" Kevin could only nod. Peter, satisfied that he was in the right, nodded his head too.

The following week, not shockingly, Kevin found himself listening once again to Peter's soundtrack, "My brother drives me crazy," on their run. When their pace finally slowed and Kevin could catch his breath, he confronted his friend. "What happens when you don't call him on it?"

Peter looked up, "What do you mean?"

"Hey, his bullshit frustrates me too. I'm just wondering what happens when you don't say anything."

"I know. He's impossible. But there's nothing I can do."

"Dude, really? Nothing? You're like a brother to me, and not the Eric kind," he teased. "How long you gonna let this go before you do something about it? I'd be a jerk to listen to you week after week and not say something. I can't be silent and have you think I think it's okay. I don't want to be the friend that supports you being miserable. I want to be the friend that supports you taking action. You either gotta man up and confront him or quit whining about it. You want to take action, I'm here. You want to figure out what to do, I'm your wingman. You want to complain, I'm done listening. No brother should be gettin' away with what he's gettin' away with."

Go Kevin! *He* knows how to ask for what he wants. With Peter's best interests in mind, and offering to help, he refuses to be a doormat and requests that his buddy's whining stops. Hello, my readers, are you noticing what just happened? Kevin's got a wand, and he knows how to use it! (Yes, I know what that sounds like. Get your mind out of the gutter and return your focus to figuring out how to ask for what *you* want.)

While it's absolutely okay to have a safe place to vent, it's not okay to use venting in lieu of asking. I get it, you need your posse. However, if your posse prevents you from taking action, if they thwart you from asking directly and specifically for what you want and from whom you want it, your posse is a prophylactic for getting you what you want.

"He's always been the baby," Peter mumbled.

"Well, that story may have worked when he *was* a baby,"

Kevin replied, "but his butt is a heck of a lot bigger now, and you need to kick him in it. Show him some tough love."

"I don't even know where to start," Peter admitted.

"Let's role-play. You be your punk-ass brother, and I'll be you."

GET WHAT YOU WANT: IMPLEMENT YOUR LINES

First, set your boundaries.

- What are your negotiables?
- What are your non-negotiables?
- What might you need to say no to? Which means you're saying yes to...?

Second, when you make an offer or request, you create an energetic and action-focused shift.

- What might I offer to myself?
- What might I offer to them?
- What might I request from myself?
- What might I request from them?
- What are the best next steps I can take to sustain the momentum of this conversation?

- What are the best next steps they can take to sustain the momentum of this conversation?

Third, set yourself up for success by preparing and practicing.

- Do I know my key "lines," questions, and flow so I can keep the conversation on track?
- What might they say or do in response to each of my main points?
- How will I respond to each of these possible scenarios?
- How might I best respond if I get blindsided with new information or a very unexpected response?
- Have I rehearsed enough to feel as confident and prepared as possible?

Knowing your lines, both what to say and where to draw them, gets easier with practice. Rehearse enough and, over time, your performance as a brilliant communicator will be naturally award-worthy. The award, of course, will be getting precisely what you want.

FINAL WORDS ON GETTING WHAT YOU WANT

My dear Wanters,

Wanting itself will never be your problem. Your wants keep you alive. From eating and procreating to working and vacationing, your wants can lead to your suffering, or they can be the driver of an energy that's channeled for impact. To reduce the former and increase the latter, I ask you, *How are you relating to your wanting?*

First, it's important to recognize and accept the presence of your wanting self. Give yourself permission to experience your wants without pushing any of them away or acting on them impulsively. When you are neither desperate in your wanting nor resistant to your wants, you can untangle the web of all your desires and see the underlying needs. When your deepest needs are satisfied, you will experience your greatest sense of fulfillment. A magical moment, indeed.

Second, if your wants are so habitually compulsive that you cannot be fully present and enjoy the moment at hand, then your obsessive wanting will get in your way. You'll be so preoccupied with wanting someone to call, wanting the presentation to go smoothly, wanting to finish the draft, wanting to be at the other party, wanting someone to change, wanting to be liked, or wanting to be rich that you'll miss the joy of all your current fulfilled wants that are right in front of you. Remain present for yourself. Everything in life is constantly shifting and evolving. Your body, the seasons, your environment, your moods, so you mistakenly move your wanting into the next hour, the next day, the next month, the next year, hoping that when your wants are fulfilled in the future, you will be happier. Ironically, it merely reinforces the feeling that you are missing something in the here and now.

Third, on the days that you do not get what you want, remind yourself that your surface wants will come and go. If you cling to them, you'll be strangely frustrated at how so few of them come to pass. If you assign profound meaning to a denied want, you'll be overly distraught. You'll know when you no longer own your wants, but your wants own you. It'll be that exact moment when one of them finally materializes, and no sooner do you get it than you dismiss it so you can focus on your next want.

Fourth, the moment you free yourself from *how* it's all supposed to go and how you might feel later on when certain wants are met or unmet, the sooner you get what you want in the here and now. Many people believe they will be happier when they get the freedom they want. They say they'll be more content when they get the lifestyle they want. They'll feel more secure when they get all the money they want. The truth is that getting what you want will not guarantee you these feelings. If you're not happy, free, content, and secure right here, right now, what makes you think you'll feel this way over there? Feeling happy, free, content, and secure has nothing to do with the money in your wallet or the size of your bank account. It's a reflection of your relationship with yourself.

Fifth, you may not get all of what you want in an initial conversation. There will be times when you make an offer or request and it is declined. Not everything you want and ask for will appear like a wish granted from a genie. Patience, grasshopper. You're planting seeds. If you tend to them and let them grow, you will eventually get what you want, or get a whole lot less of what you don't want. Over time, your expectations may even shift. This shift can influence and change what you want or amend how you want it. As you modify your wants, over time you can reap the rewards from new offers and requests. You can still establish your own boundaries, set new rules, disengage, change the way you play the game, implement a magical phrase, or figure out an alternative approach to getting what you want. Most importantly, follow your words with action. Taking action generates the energy you need to get you what it is you want. You won't always plant, harvest, and reap all in one conversation, so harness your energy and plan to work the whole season if this want of yours means so much to you.

Dwelling on your disappointment for too long will not move you in the direction of your desires. You cannot force help on anyone nor demand that your expectations be instantly fulfilled. In most conversations, you'll have at least ignited your boss's, a friend's, a partner's, or your own mind to start working on what you want. Being told no doesn't warm the cockles of your heart; just ask any toddler. Unlike a toddler, though, you don't get to throw yourself down and wail. (Alright, if you insist, set the timer for four minutes. Rant. Rave. Whine. Complain. Flail around. Hit a pillow. Down a shot. Pout. Ding! Ding! Oh my, time's up already?! Good, now it's time to grow a pair.) Perseverance, who, by the way, is first cousins with determination, grit, and doggedness, is what you need to send your tenacious tushy back out into the world so you may wag it with confidence.

Knowing that your life unfolds one conversation at a time and believing in your ability to turn a tough conversation into a highly profitable one means your potential is limitless.

The next time you find yourself asking, *How do I get what I want?* remember to use your wand. Your wand knows that the very best way to answer this question is by loving, accepting, and respecting yourself and honoring the worth of your own voice. One conversation at a time.

ACKNOWLEDGMENTS

First and foremost, a huge thank you to each and every person who took the time to get the concepts, get my voice, and get my passion for sharing these steps so others can *Get It* too. This book would not have seen the light of day without numerous conversations—funny, tough, raw, intense, silly and supportive—along the way. Thank you to the team at Scribe Media for being brilliantly creative and incredibly efficient. I felt like I was in very good hands from day one. Thanks to my coaching and consulting clients who embraced these tools over the years and proved they really do work by creating extraordinarily profitable, happier and more fulfilling lives. Thanks to Mandy who is a gifted editor. She endured multiple readings. Thanks to my LadyBallz Mastermind—Jenny, Katie, and Susan—who are pillars of support and speak their own beautiful love language. Thanks to my parents who so generously took the time to share their keen insights and encouraged me to honor my own voice. Thanks to Omar, who proves that once you *Get It*, you really, really do get what your heart desires. Last but not least, thank you dear readers. Every time you show up to a conversation willing and ready to honor the worth of your own voice, magical things happen. Hugs.